Essential Elements of
Business Information Systems

Brian Corr BSc

Brian Corr is currently a lecturer in Computing at South Birmingham College with wide experience of teaching on undergraduate level courses. He has worked for many years in industry as a Systems Analyst for leading financial, information services and retail organisations.

Series adviser: Bob Cudmore BEd, MBA, Head of Management and Professional Studies Division, South Birmingham College

Technical adviser: Teresa Heywood BA, Section Head of Computing, South Birmingham College

Published in association with South Birmingham College
DP Publications Ltd
1995

Acknowledgments

For my parents, Margaret and Hugh.

A CIP catalogue reference for this book is available from the British Library

ISBN 1 85805 136 3

Copyright © Brian Corr, 1995

All rights reserved
No part of this publication may be reproduced, stored in a retrieval system, or transmitted in any form or by any means, electronic, mechanical, photocopying, recording, or otherwise, without the prior permission of the copyright owner.

Typeset by
   Nigel Jordan, Fareham
   KAI Typesetting, Nottingham

Printed in Great Britain by the Guernsey Press Co. Ltd, Vale, Guernsey

Preface

Aim

The aim of the *Essential Elements* series is to provide course support material covering the main subject areas of HND/C Business Studies and equivalent level courses at a price that students can afford. Students can select titles to suit the requirements of their own particular courses whether BTEC Certificate in Business Administration, Certificate in Marketing, IPS Foundation, Institute of Bankers, Access to Business Studies, Institute of Personnel Management, or other appropriate undergraduate and professional courses.

Many courses now have a modular structure, i.e. individual subjects are taught in a relatively short period of, say, 10 to 12 weeks. The *Essential Elements* series meets the need for material which can be built into the students' study programmes and used for directed self-study. All the texts, therefore, include activities with answers for students' self-assessment, activities for lecturer-assessment, and references to further reading.

The series is a joint venture between DP Publications and South Birmingham College.

How to use the series

All the books in the series are intended to be used as workbooks and provide approximately 70 hours of study material. Each text covers the essential elements of that subject, so that the core of any course at this level is covered, leaving the lecturer to add supplementary material if required. All have the following features:

- **In-text activities,** which aim to promote understanding of the principles, and are set at frequent intervals in the text. The solutions add to the student's knowledge, as well as providing an introduction to the next learning point.

- **End of chapter exercises,** some of which are intended for self-assessment by the student (these have solutions at the back of the book). Others are suitable for setting by the lecturer and answers or marking guides are provided in the Lecturers' Supplement. These exercises include progress and review questions, multiple choice questions, which test specific knowledge and allow rapid marking, practice questions, questions for advanced students, and assignments.

- **Further reading references** for students who wish to follow up particular topics in more depth.

- **Lecturers' Supplement,** which is available free of charge to lecturers adopting the book as a course text. It includes answers or guides to marking to help with student assessment.

Other titles in the series

Available now: Business Economics, Business Statistics, Quantitative Methods, Management Accounting, Marketing, Financial Accounting, Human Resource Management.

Available 1996: Business Law, Total Quality Management.

Contents

Preface	iii

1 Information and Information Systems
1.1	Introduction	1
1.2	Information	1
1.3	Information systems	3
1.4	Transaction Processing Systems (TPS)	6
1.5	Management Information Systems (MIS)	7
1.6	Office Automation Systems (OAS)	9
1.7	Decision Support Systems (DSS)	9
1.8	Executive Information Systems (EIS)	12
1.9	Summary	13
	Further reading, exercises, assignment	13

2 Elements of Computer Systems
2.1	Introduction	16
2.2	Components of computer systems	16
2.3	Input devices and data capture	20
2.4	Data validation	22
2.5	Output devices	25
2.6	Data storage devices	26
2.7	Telecommunications and networks	29
2.8	Summary	32
	Further reading, exercises, assignment	32

3 File Systems and Database Systems
3.1	Introduction	36
3.2	The traditional file system	36
3.3	Database concepts	39
3.4	Advantages of Databases	41
3.5	The Entity-Relationship diagram	43
3.6	Normalisation	46
3.7	Building the physical database	49
3.8	Summary	52
	Further reading, exercises, assignment	52

4 Developing Information Systems

4.1	Introduction	56
4.2	Roles in systems development	56
4.3	The Systems Development Life Cycle	57
4.4	Project definition and feasibility study	60
4.5	Systems analysis	61
4.6	Systems design	64
4.7	Programming	65
4.8	Implementation	66
4.9	Prototyping	68
4.10	Summary	69
	Further reading, exercises, assignment	69

5 Systems Analysis Techniques

5.1	Introduction	73
5.2	Process analysis	73
5.3	Data Flow Diagrams (DFD)	77
5.4	Data dictionary	80
5.5	Entity life histories	81
5.6	Decision tables	84
5.7	Summary	86
	Further reading, exercises, assignment	86

6 Detailed Systems Design

6.1	Introduction	90
6.2	Code design	90
6.3	Diaglogue design	92
6.4	Screen design	96
6.5	Function design	100
6.6	Summary	103
	Further reading, exercises, assignment	103

Answers to Progress Questions — 107

Index — 111

1 Information and Information Systems

1.1 Introduction

This chapter defines the term information and explains the different types of information systems which are found in organisations. On completion of this chapter you should be able to:

- explain the qualities of good information;
- identify the components of an information system;
- understand the role and characteristics of a Transaction Processing System (TPS);
- understand the role and characteristics of a Management Information System (MIS);
- understand the role and characteristics of an Office Automation System (OAS);
- understand the role and characteristics of a Decision Support System (DSS);
- understand the role and characteristics of an Executive Information System (EIS);

1.2 Information

The terms data and information are often used interchangeably but, in fact, they have different meanings, and it is important to be able to distinguish between them. Data refers to the basic facts which are collected and recorded in a database or in a computer file system. For example, an organisation's Personnel Department would record data about each employee including their name, address, sex, job title, annual salary, hours worked, tax code, national insurance number etc. Information, however, is defined as data which has been processed in order to convey meaning to the person who receives it. For example, the data on employees may be input to a computer program which processes it in order to calculate information on the number of employees, the number of male and female employees, the total salary of all employees and the average salary of an employee.

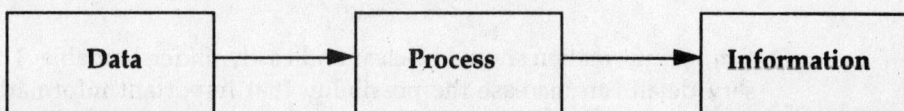

Information is needed by managers to assist them to perform the main functions of management, which are:

- forecasting;
- planning;
- organising;
- co-ordinating;
- decision making;
- controlling.

In order to perform these functions effectively management may require information from a number of sources both internal and external to the organisation. Most internal information will be obtained from the data held on the organisation's database. External information will be obtained from sources outside the organisation such as market research, research and development work, new government legislation etc. Irrespective of whether the information is internal or external, there are a number of qualities which it must have in order to be of use to management.

> **Activity**
>
> Identify the main qualities which information should possess in order to be of use to management.

Information should have the following qualities:

- *Accuracy*: it is more likely that management will make the correct decision if the information upon which the decision is based is accurate. There are different levels of accuracy which may be possible and the manager who requests the information should also specify the level of accuracy that is required. In many cases, absolute accuracy is not necessary. For example, a Sales Manager may only require information on the value of monthly sales to the nearest thousand pounds and not to the nearest penny. In general, the greater the level of accuracy, the greater the cost of producing the information.

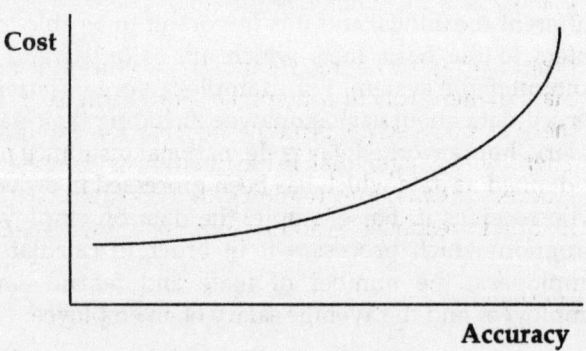

- *Clarity*: information should be clear and easily understandable. Too much unnecessary detail can increase the possibility that important information may be overlooked. The recipient of information should only be provided with the information which meets their exact needs. For example, if the Principal of a college requires a regular end of term report showing the number of students in each faculty, then there is no need to provide additional information such as the number of students by gender, by ethnic origin, by course etc. The level of detail that is required will vary with the level of management which is using the information. In general, the higher the level of management then the less detail that is required.

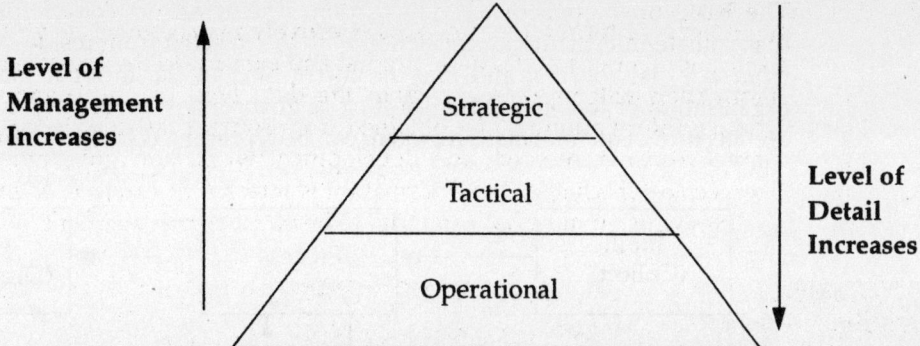

- *Timeliness*: information must be produced and communicated in time for it to be used effectively by management. Some decisions need to be taken quickly and therefore the information which could influence the decision must be produced quickly also. If the information arrives after the decision has been made then it is of no value. A problem with many of the information systems developed before the introduction of databases, is that they are inflexible and it is often very difficult to produce new information quickly. The use of a database for storing an organisation's data increases flexibility and the ability to produce information quickly. Very little training would be required for a manager to be able to interrogate a database, using a query language, and obtain the information required, without needing to involve systems analysts or programmers.

- *Relevance*: information must be relevant to the level of management which receives it and to the nature of the decisions which they may need to take. Information which is appropriate for managers at one level will not be appropriate for managers at the other levels.

- *Frequency*: information should be produced at an appropriate frequency for the management function involved. For example, if decisions are taken monthly then there is no need to produce information for those decisions on a weekly basis. There is a danger that if information is produced too frequently then it may be ignored. Ideally, information systems should facilitate the easy production of information in response to ad hoc requests from management.

1.3 Information Systems

The term 'information system' refers to any computer-based system which is used to assist in the management and operation of an organisation. Information systems may be used in any of the following ways:

- to increase the efficiency and effectiveness of the business operations of an organisation;

- to enable management to more effectively control the operations of an organisation;

- to improve the effectiveness of management decision making;

- to facilitate the co-ordination of activities within an organisation.

The basic operations of an information system are to collect, process, store and disseminate information. Information may be collected from inside the organisation or from external sources, and may be distributed to the internal management of the organisation or to external bodies such as government regulatory agencies. The basic architecture of an information system can be represented by the following diagram:

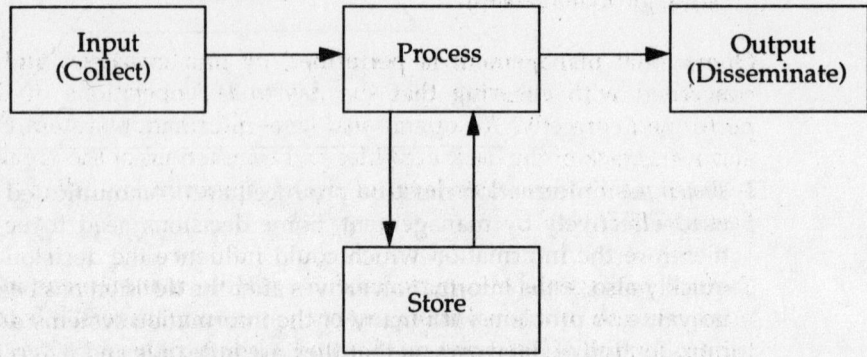

In a large organisation there will be many information systems serving different functions and different levels of management within the organisation. Information will flow between the different information systems such that the output from one system may become the input to another system, or the information stored by one system may be used as input to another system. To demonstrate this, consider the Ordering, Warehouse and Accounts functions of an organisation. Each function will have its own information system and will store data related to its own activities. The following steps describe what is taking place in the diagram:

i. An order is received from a customer and its details are recorded.

ii. Details of the order are passed to the Warehouse.

iii. The Warehouse sends the goods to the customer, updates the status of the order, updates its own warehouse data to show the reduction in stock level, and notifies Accounts that the order has been fulfilled.

iv. Accounts send an invoice to the customer, updates the status of the order and updates its own customer accounts data.

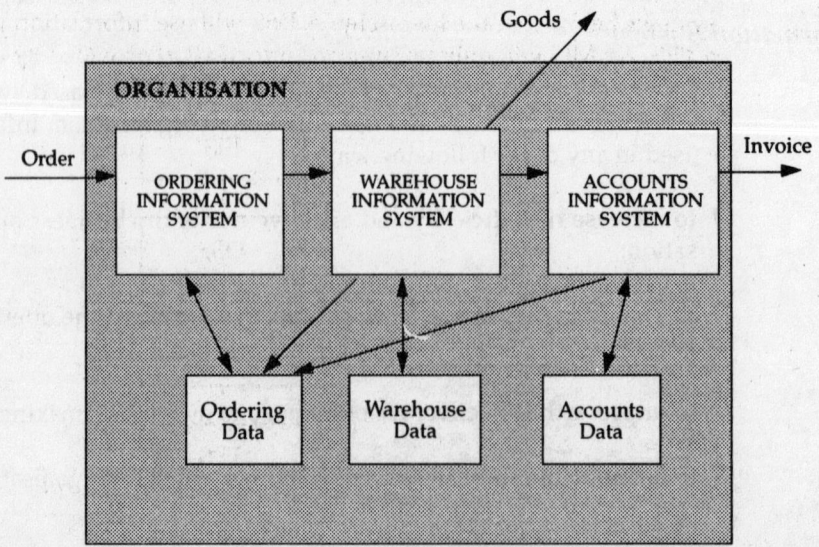

There are three levels of management within an organisation, which have specific information requirements and which are served by different types of information system:
- operational management;
- tactical management;
- strategic management.

Operational management is performed by line managers and supervisors and is concerned with ensuring that the day-to-day operations of the organisation are performed correctly. An operational-level information system will have to facilitate and keep track of the basic activities and transactions of the organisation. Information systems which serve this level of the organisation are called *Transaction Processing Systems (TPS)*.

Tactical management is performed by middle management including department managers and functional managers such as sales managers. It is concerned with monitoring, controlling, decision making and administration activities related to the performance of the operational units of the organisation. *Management Information Systems (MIS)* concentrate on the regular reporting of the transactions of the organisation, therefore facilitating monitoring and control. They are most commonly used at this level, but may also be used at the operational and strategic levels.

Strategic management is performed by the senior management of the organisation, such as the Board of Directors, and is concerned with the setting of strategic objectives and long term planning. Decisions at this level will be based on information which attempts to predict the future of the organisation and its environment. The main concern is to match the organisation to the predicted future environment. *Decision Support Systems (DSS)* support nonroutine decision making for which information requirements may not be clear. They are used widely, though not exclusively, at this level. *Executive Information Systems (EIS)* which combine decision support, communications and graphics facilities are currently under development for senior management use.

The relationship between these systems is demonstrated by the following diagram. An EIS, which is the highest level system, will use information provided by each of the systems below it in the hierarchy. A DSS will use information provided by an MIS and a TPS. An MIS will only use internal information provided by a TPS.

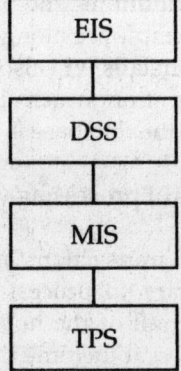

The final type of information system which is considered is an *Office Automation System (OAS)*. An OAS is used to enhance the performance of the administration function in an organisation and includes facilities for word processing, electronic mail and others. It does not readily fit into a specific management level as administration is an organisation-wide function.

Each functional area of a large organisation may have its own operational, tactical and strategic level systems. For example, the sales function will have an operational-level sales system to process sales orders and record all of the daily sales. Reports on the monthly sales figures for each area and each product will be produced by a tactical-level system, and a strategic-level system will attempt to forecast sales trends for the next five years.

1.4 Transaction Processing Systems (TPS)

As the name suggests, TPS are used to process all of the routine transactions generated by the main operations of an organisation. Each of the major functional areas of an organisation, such as marketing, production and personnel will have a TPS. A good example of a TPS is that used by financial services organisations such as banks and building societies for recording all deposits and withdrawals against customer accounts. Each deposit and withdrawal is regarded as a transaction which will be processed against the account to produce the correct account balance.

A TPS is the main system through which information is stored on an organisation's database. Consequently, it is the main source of information for the other types of information systems.

Activity

Describe three types of TPS which you may encounter.

A college or university will have a system to record student enrolments, where each enrolment is treated as a transaction with details recorded in a database. Student records will then need to be maintained and further transactions will be generated when a student withdraws from a course, transfers to another course, or changes personal details such as address or phone number.

In a payroll system, transactions are generated containing the details of the employee and the number of hours which they have worked each day during the payment period. These transactions are then processed against details of the rate of pay, pension contributions and tax contributions of each employee. Payslips are produced for each employee along with details of the employees' accounts to be credited. The employee details will also be updated to reflect the salary paid to date.

An airline reservation system is a TPS in which a transaction is created for each booking made, and the database is immediately updated to reflect the new booking.

There are two types of processing which may occur in a TPS:

- *Batch Processing*: transactions are stored and accumulated until the time when it becomes necessary to process them. For example, a payroll system is a batch system in which all of the hours worked by an employee are accumulated until they are processed at the time the payroll needs to be produced.

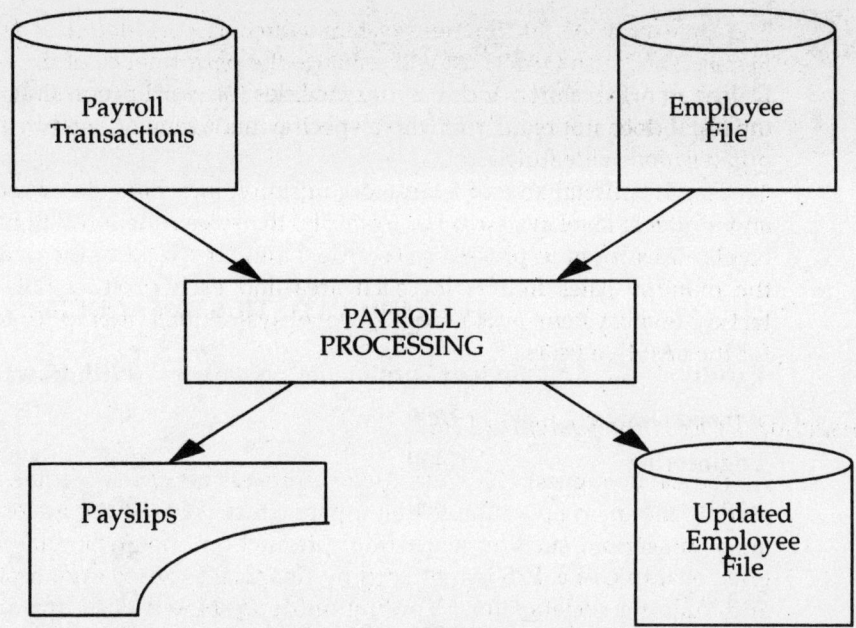

❐ *On-line Processing*: transactions are processed immediately and the database is updated to reflect the new situation. For example, an airline reservation system is an on-line system in which, once a booking has been made the database is updated to show that the places booked are no longer available on the flight.

American Airlines were the first to develop an on-line airline reservation system which allowed customers to quickly see flight availability and to book flights via terminals in travel agent offices. The implementation of this system gave American Airlines an advantage over their competitors who were forced to follow suit.

1.5 Management Information Systems (MIS)

MIS are designed to assist management, at all levels of the organisation, to control the functions for which they are responsible. MIS generally achieve this through the regular production of summarised reports of the transactions which have taken place in the organisation. For example, an airline reservations system may have an MIS to produce monthly reports showing the number of tickets sold to specific destinations. MIS usually rely on existing internal data, generated by TPS, to produce information. In some cases they do use information obtained from external sources.

The information that is produced by an MIS may be used by management for a number of purposes, including:

❐ to control the operations of the organisation;

❐ to assist with decision making at the operational and tactical levels of management;

❐ to assist with planning at the senior management level.

> **Activity**
>
> Define an MIS report which may be produced by a college or university to indicate the number of student enrolments, withdrawals and retention rates in each faculty.

Date: 12 April 1995

STUDENT STATISTICS BY FACULTY

Faculty	Number of Enrolments	Number of Withdrawals	Retention Rate
Art and Design	1000	50	95%
Engineering	1400	100	93%
Languages	850	30	96%
Law	300	40	87%
Science	1200	60	95%
Total	4750	280	94%

Some MIS reports are only produced when exceptional conditions occur. This is known as exception reporting. For example, it may be decided that the above report should only be produced when the number of withdrawals in a faculty exceeds the figure 100. In this case, the report would be known as an 'exception report'.

Many MIS are now being developed, which provide facilities for managers to perform ad hoc enquiries on data and produce their own reports whenever necessary. This area is known as end-user computing and refers to users being able to build their own information systems, in this case an MIS, without referring to systems analysts or programmers. End-user computing tools include spreadsheet packages such as Microsoft Excel, database packages such as Microsoft Access, and database query languages such as SQL (Structured Query Language).

With an end-user computing tool such as Microsoft Excel, the user could produce a graph of the information contained in the report above, such as the bar chart below which shows the retention rate of each faculty.

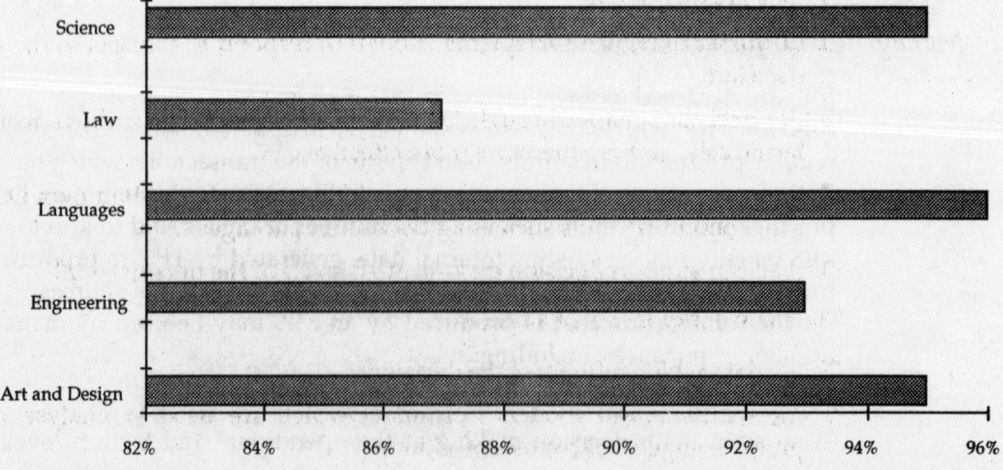

Bar Chart of Retention Rate by Faculty

1.6 Office Automation Systems (OAS)

OAS allow the creation, storage and communication of information in written, verbal or video form throughout an organisation and between organisations. The components of an OAS may include any combination of the following:

- Word Processor to create documents electronically;
- Electronic Mail to send and receive messages;
- Facsimile to transmit documents over telephone lines;
- Voice Mail to allow the storing and forwarding of spoken messages;
- Image Processing to allow documents and pictures to be stored on computer;
- Video-Conferencing to allow people to communicate face-to-face while at different locations;
- Multimedia systems which allow the combination of text, graphics, images, animation and sound.

It is important that an organisation co-ordinates the purchase of its OAS software and hardware to ensure compatibility throughout the organisation. For example, it is advantageous for each department to use the same word processing package as this allows the easy transferral of files between departments and also enables staff to be immediately productive if transferred between departments.

The technology associated with OAS is developing rapidly and it is important for an organisation to be aware of new developments. However, an organisation must be careful to choose the most appropriate time to upgrade its software, as it will not wish to invest in something which may become quickly outdated.

1.7 Decision Support Systems (DSS)

DSS are interactive systems which use data and mathematical models to assist decision making. They are designed for senior management decision making, although managers at all levels may find them useful. The main objective of a DSS is to improve the effectiveness of decisions. DSS have the following characteristics and benefits:

- they can be used to solve complex problems;
- they can provide a fast response to unexpected situations;
- they are interactive;
- they are flexible and adaptable enough to respond to changes to the elements of a decision;
- the decisions made through DSS are more objective than those which are made intuitively, and are therefore more effective;
- they are easy to build, and users should be able to build their own DSS using end-user computing tools such as a spreadsheet package;
- they can support decision making at all levels of the organisation.

The main components of a DSS are:

- the data which influences the decision;
- the mathematical models (formulae) which are used to analyse the data and produce suggested courses of action;
- the dialogue between the user and the system.

The architecture of a DSS can be shown as follows:

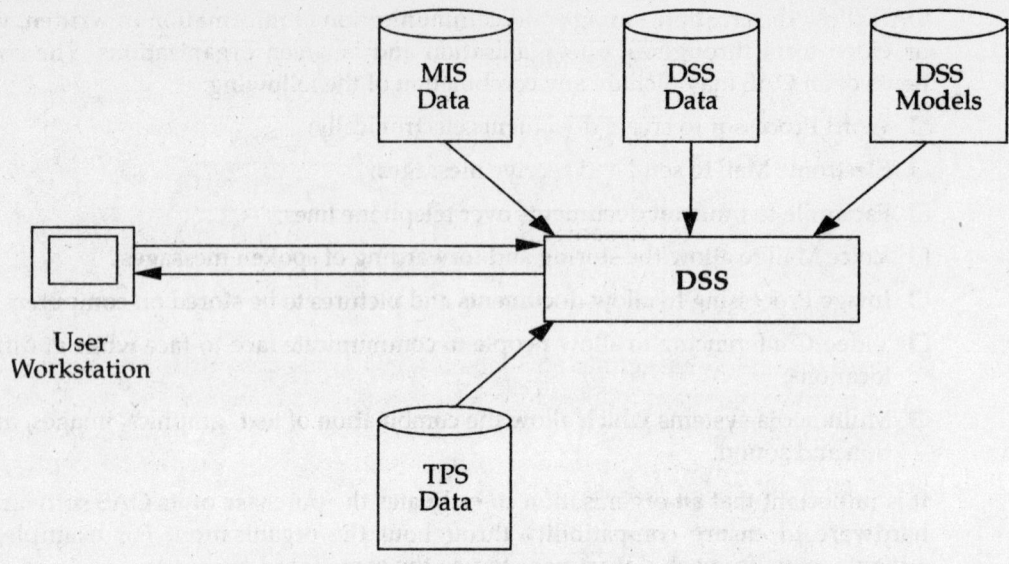

Activity

Describe how you could build a DSS to help you decide which car to purchase.

The data for the DSS would consist of all of the data which is collected on the cars between which a choice is to be made. For example, data might be collected on the attributes, car model, price, acceleration, top speed and fuel economy from a variety of car magazines and manufacturer's information. Examples of this data might be:

Make/Model	Price	Acceleration (0-60)	Top Speed (mpg)	Fuel Economy
Rover 100 1.4 GSi	£10,281	10.7	103	56
Nissan Micra 1.3 SLX	£10,410	12.0	106	58
Renault Clio 1.4 RT	£10,395	11.3	109	57
Vauxhall Corsa 1.6 GSi	£12,220	9.0	121	53

A mathematical model could then be constructed which applies a weighting to each car within each attribute. For example, the car with the best acceleration would have a weighting of 1.0, the car with the worst acceleration would have a weighting of 0.1, and the other weightings would be applied proportionately.

Make/Model	Price Weighting	Acceleration Weighting	Top Speed Weighting	Economy Weighting
Rover 100 1.4 GSi	1.0	0.61	0.1	0.64
Nissan Micra 1.3 SLX	0.94	0.1	0.25	1.0
Renault Clio 1.4 RT	0.95	0.79	0.4	0.82
Vauxhall Corsa 1.6 GSi	0.1	1.0	1.0	0.1

A second formula could then be applied to find the overall rating of each model. In this case an average rating has been calculated.

Make/Model	Average Weighting
Rover 100 1.4 GSi	0.59
Nissan Micra 1.3 SLX	0.57
Renault Clio 1.4 RT	0.74
Vauxhall Corsa 1.6 GSi	0.55

If the user decides that certain attributes are more important than others, for example price is most important followed by acceleration, fuel economy and top speed, then the attributes themselves can be given ratings, and these can then be included in a formula to give overall ratings. For example, the following are the attribute weightings which have been chosen:

Attribute	Weighting
Price	2.0
Acceleration	1.7
Top Speed	1.2
Fuel Economy	1.5

These are then applied to each respective weighting for each model by simply multiplying each weighting by the attribute weighting.

Make/Model	Price Weighting	Acceleration Weighting	Top Speed Weighting	Economy Weighting
Rover 100 1.4 GSi	2.0	1.04	0.12	0.96
Nissan Micra 1.3 SLX	1.88	0.17	0.3	1.5
Renault Clio 1.4 RT	1.9	1.34	0.48	1.23
Vauxhall Corsa 1.6 GSi	0.2	1.7	1.2	0.15

The average weighting of each is then calculated, using the same formula as before.

Make/Model	Average Weighting
Rover 100 1.4 GSi	1.03
Nissan Micra 1.3 SLX	0.96
Renault Clio 1.4 RT	1.24
Vauxhall Corsa 1.6 GSi	0.81

The above DSS could be built on a spreadsheet package such as Microsoft Excel or Lotus 1-2-3. These packages are also known as DSS generators, which also include integrated packages such as Microsoft Office which combine spreadsheet, database and graphics packages. A DSS generator provides the capability of building a DSS quickly, easily and cheaply.

1.8 Executive Information Systems (EIS)

EIS are also known as Executive Support Systems (ESS). They are an attempt to provide senior executives with an information system which they will use themselves. Often, executives do not use DSS themselves, but request professional assistants to do so to find out information on their behalf.

An EIS is an extension of a DSS, and is basically a tracking and control system which attempts to keep executives aware of what is happening in important areas related to their organisation. These areas may be internal or external to the organisation. Internal information will be obtained from the other information systems of the organisation, TPS, MIS and DSS. External information may include things like economic indicators and exchange rates.

An EIS provides information which executives need to perform their day to day duties and responsibilities. The information is provided in a user-friendly and easy to understand format, usually graphical. The user will be able to look at the information to the level of detail required. For example, a summary report may be provided at company level, from this the user can choose to proceed to division level and then department level, revealing more detail at each level.

The characteristics of EIS are:

❐ mainly used for monitoring and control;

❐ tailored to the individual style of the executive;

❐ provide graphics capabilities;

❐ user-friendly;

❐ provide access to timely information;

❐ provide OAS facilities such as electronic mail and voice mail.

The architecture of an EIS can be shown as follows:

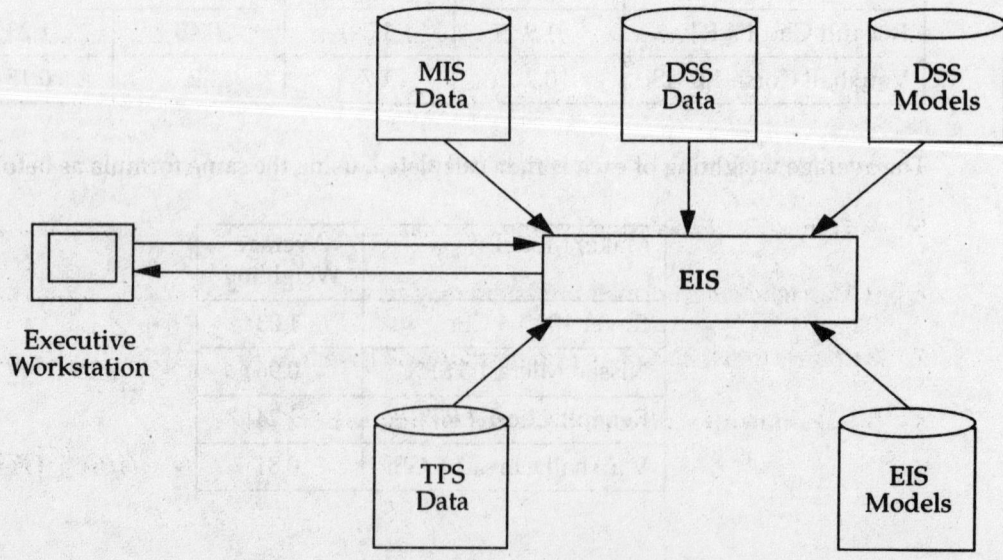

1.9 Summary

In this chapter we have looked at the definition of information and the qualities of good information. You have examined the concept of information systems and seen how they may be related to the different functional areas and management levels of an organisation. You have identified the main types of information system and the characteristics and role of each. You have seen that TPS handle the main business operations of an organisation and are a source of information for the other information systems. You have identified that MIS are concerned with the regular reporting of information from internal sources, and may be used by all levels of management. You have identified the components of an OAS. You have seen that DSS are mainly used by senior management to improve the effectiveness of decisions. You have also noted that EIS are an attempt to provide senior executives with an information system which meets their information requirements, provides decision support and the facilities of an OAS.

Further reading

Lucey, Terry, *Management Information Systems*, DP Publications

Clifton, H.D., *Business Information Systems*, Prentice Hall

Laudon, K.C. & Laudon, J.P., *Management Information Systems*, Macmillan

Kroenke & Hatch, *Management Information Systems*, McGraw-Hill

Exercises

Progress questions

These questions have been designed to help you remember the key points in this chapter. The answers are given at the back of the book.

Complete the following sentences:

1. Information can be defined as ....

2. Information is needed to..

3. The qualities of good information are ....

4. An information system can be defined as..

5. A Transaction Processing System ....

6. A Management Information System may serve..

7. Each functional area of an organisation will have..

8. Information must be communicated on time to be of value.

    True ☐ False ☐

9. A Transaction Processing System is used at the tactical-level of an organisation.

    True ☐ False ☐

10. Decision Support Systems are used to solve routine problems.

    True ☐ False ☐

Review questions

These questions have been designed to help you check your comprehension of the key points in this chapter. You may wish to look further than the text in this chapter to answer them fully. You can check your answers by referring to the appropriate section.

11. Explain the main differences between the terms data and information. (Section 1.2)

12. Explain what is meant by 'batch processing'. (Section 1.4)

13. Explain what is meant by 'exception reporting'. (Section 1.5)

14. Identify the features of an Office Automation System. (Section 1.6)

Multiple choice questions

The answers to these questions will be given in the Lecturer's Supplement.

15. The basic data about an organisation's business is generated by:
    a) TPS
    b) OAS
    c) MIS
    d) none of the above

16. DSS are used by:
    a) strategic management only
    b) strategic and tactical management only
    c) operational management only
    d) all levels of management

17. Regular formatted reports are provided by:
    a) EIS
    b) MIS
    c) OAS
    d) TPS

18. Flexibility and adaptability are features of:
    a) TPS
    b) EIS
    c) DSS
    d) MIS

1 Information and Information Systems

Practice questions

A marking guide to these questions will be given in the Lecturer's Supplement.

19. Describe a situation for which on-line processing would be appropriate.

20. Explain the functions of an OAS.

21. Describe the differences between a TPS and an MIS.

22. Describe the characteristics of a DSS.

Questions for advanced students

A marking guide to these questions will be given in the Lecturer's Supplement.

23. Describe the differences between a DSS and an MIS.

24. Explain the relationships between the major types of information systems in an organisation.

Assignment

Investigate an organisation in your local area and obtain information on the following types of information systems used:
i. Transaction Processing Systems (TPS)
ii. Management Information Systems (MIS)
iii. Decision Support Systems (DSS)

Produce a report which describes the following:
i. what each system does within the organisation;
ii. the inputs, processing and outputs of each system;
iii. the level of management within the organisation which uses each system. For the MIS, indicate the frequency and nature of reports which are produced. For the DSS, indicate the nature of the decisions which are assisted by the use of the DSS.

Give brief examples of the data processed and the information produced by each system. Describe, using an example, how the information produced by one system can be used as input to another system.

2 Elements of Computer Systems

2.1 Introduction

This chapter examines the different elements which comprise a computer system. On completion of this chapter you should be able to:

- identify the main components which comprise a computer system;
- describe the different input devices available for data capture;
- describe the methods used for data validation;
- describe the different output devices available;
- describe the different storage media available, and understand the different methods of gaining access to the data;
- understand the basics of telecommunications and computer networks.

2.2 Components of Computer Systems

Within any computer system, the main components fall into one of two categories:

- *Hardware*: the physical devices which make up the computer system;
- *Software*: the computer programs which are executed within the computer.

The collection of hardware devices which make up the computer system can be referred to as:

- *Input Devices*: allow data to be entered into the computer system.
- *Output Devices*: produce output from the computer system.
- *Storage Devices*: allow data to be stored for use by the computer system.
- *Central Processing Unit (CPU)*: the actual part of the computer which performs all of the processing.
- *Communications Devices*: allow one computer to communicate with another computer.

Activity

Give two actual examples of each of the following:
- input devices;
- output devices;
- storage devices;
- communications devices.

The most common and obvious examples of input devices are the keyboard and the mouse which are available with all Personal Computers. The output devices are equally obvious and they are the Visual Display Unit (VDU) and printer. Storage devices are magnetic disk and optical disk, and communications devices are modem and telephone lines.

The basic structure of a computer system which includes the above hardware is:

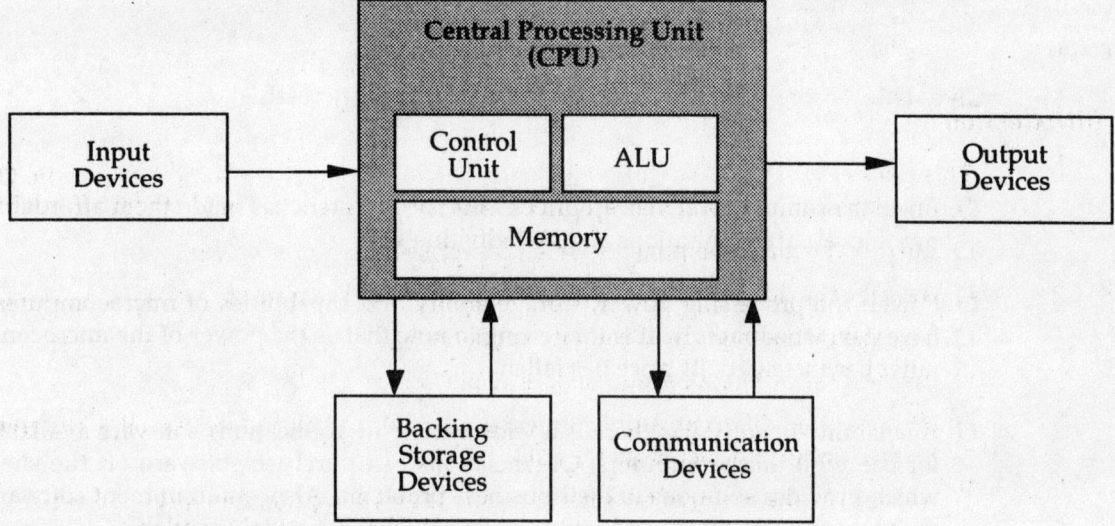

Each arrow in the above diagram represents the transfer of data. For example, data is transferred from the input device to the CPU.

The elements of the CPU are:

- *Control Unit*: reads the program in Main Store and directs the other hardware components of the computer system to perform the tasks required by the program.

- *Arithmetic-Logic Unit (ALU)*: performs the logical and arithmetic operations of the computer.

- *Main Store (Memory)*: holds, temporarily, the program and data currently being processed by the computer. The most common type of main store is known as RAM (Random Access Memory). RAM is said to be volatile, as all data which is held in RAM is lost when the computer is switched off.

Computers can be classified according to their size and power:

- *Mainframes* are large computers which have a large main store, fast CPU and can support a large number of input, output and storage devices. Mainframes are popular with large national and multi-national organisations although, since the late 1980's the trend has been away from mainframes and towards distributed systems composed of minicomputers and microcomputers. The majority of mainframe computers are made by IBM.

- *Microcomputers* (Personal Computers) are the smallest type of computer and have seen the most rapid technological development since the mid 1980s. Microcomputers are widely used in organisations by all levels of staff from clerical level up to senior executive level. They are also widely used in universities and colleges, and are popular with home users.

- *Minicomputers* fall between mainframes and microcomputers in terms of size and power. They are smaller than mainframes and have less main store, and can support fewer input, output and storage devices. Examples of minicomputers are the DEC VAX and the IBM AS/400.

> *Activity*
>
> Give some reasons why microcomputers have been so successful.

- Price: the comparatively cheap price of microcomputers has made them affordable by all levels of organisations and by individuals.

- Power: the processing power, storage ability and capabilities of microcomputers have developed rapidly. It is interesting to note that as the power of the microcomputer has increased, its price has fallen.

- Availability of software: there is a wide variety of applications software available for use with microcomputers. Organisations can purchase software off the shelf which provides solutions to their business problems. Also, entertainment software such as computer games and multi-media software are widely available.

- Telecommunications Networks: the advances in telecommunications have allowed microcomputers to easily communicate with each other via networks. For organisations, this has meant that work can now be done locally rather than centrally. As a microcomputer has its own processor, it can be used as a stand-alone machine or connected to a mainframe or minicomputer. A terminal, however, consists only of a VDU and keyboard and is entirely dependent on the processor of the computer to which it is linked.

There are two main types of software:

i. *Applications Software*: programs which are written to perform tasks for the users of computer systems. Applications software may be purchased off the shelf to perform a common task, or it may also be written by an organisation for use only within that organisation. For example, the majority of a bank's business applications will be controlled by applications software written for the bank by its own computing staff.

ii. *Systems Software*: programs which control the way the computer operates and manages all of the components of the computer system such as printers, storage devices, memory etc. This is known as the *operating system*.

> *Activity*
>
> Identify three different types of operating systems software, and at least six different applications software packages.

Probably the most widely known operating systems software are MS-DOS, Windows and OS-2 which are used with Personal Computers. MS-DOS and Windows are supplied by Microsoft which is also the largest supplier of applications software. The most common applications software packages are those which are used for word processing, spreadsheets, databases and desktop publishing. Examples of these are Microsoft Word and WordPerfect for word processing, Microsoft Excel and Lotus 1-2-3 for spreadsheets, Microsoft Access and Borland Paradox for database, and Microsoft Publisher and Corel Ventura for desktop publishing.

The operating system provides special capabilities which allow computer systems to be used by many users at the same time:

❏ *Multiprogramming*: allows multiple programs to share a computer's resources at one time through concurrent use of the CPU. Control is switched between the programs so that when one is using the CPU, the others are engaged in input and output. The advantage of multiprogramming is that as the CPU does not have to wait for one program to finish the much slower task of input and output, the CPU is used much more effectively and the computer can perform a greater amount of processing.

❏ *Time-sharing*: in a time-sharing environment, the use of the CPU is shared out amongst a number of users. Each user is allocated a small slice of CPU time, during which they can perform the operations they require.

CPU time ─────────────────────────────────────▶

| USER 1 | USER 2 | USER 3 | USER 4 | USER 1 | USER 2 | USER 3 | USER 4 | USER 1 | USER 2 | . . . . |

❏ *Virtual Storage*: is based on the fact that only a few instructions of any program are used at a certain time. With virtual storage, the program is broken down into a number of segments. Each segment can then be called into main store only when it is required and then returned to disk. This prevents an entire program sitting in main store for the duration of its execution. It has the advantage that many more programs can be in the CPU at the same time.

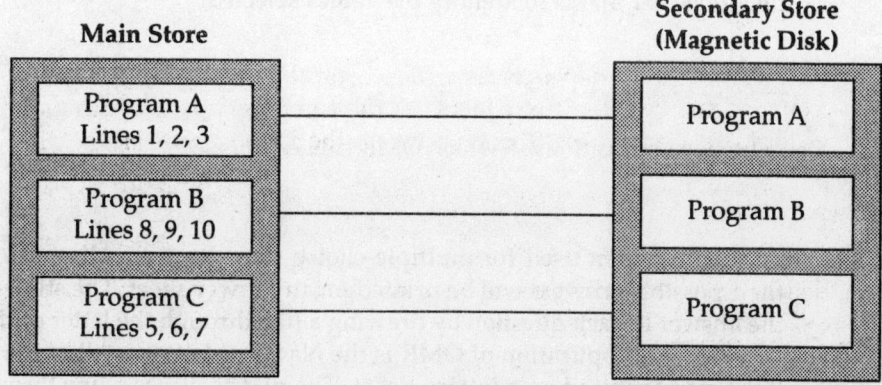

❏ *Multiprocessing*: is the use of a number of CPUs at the same time. One main CPU is connected to several work CPUs. Each work CPU handles input and output from the main CPU and co-ordinates the work of the slower input and output devices.

2.3 Input Devices and Data Capture

Input devices are those devices which are used to enter data into a computer. The most obvious examples of input devices are the keyboard and the mouse. The process by which an input device accepts data and converts it into a computer-sensible form is known as *data capture*. Data capture can be performed by two means:

- Manual data entry by which a user enters the data via an input device such as a keyboard.
- Automated data entry by which an input device reads the data at its source.

> **Activity**
>
> What are the disadvantages of data capture via a keyboard?

Data capture which involves a user reading a source document and entering the data into a computer has the following disadvantages:

- time-consuming, particularly when a large amount of data must be input;
- costly, due to the labour needed to collect and input the data;
- error prone as transcription errors are more likely to occur.

Most manual data entry is done using on-line systems, in which the user and the computer interact. A data entry screen will be presented to the user for completion. The screen should be laid out in a similar format to the document from which the data is to be read. Each item of data which the user enters can be validated for its correctness by the computer system. The use of *data validation* in on-line systems can significantly reduce the likelihood of data entry errors. See next section for details of data validation.

Automated data capture is performed by devices which read the data directly from the source document. The main methods of automated data capture are:

- *Optical Mark Reading (OMR)*: this works by the allocation of values to specific positions on a document. These positions can then be marked using a pencil or pen, and the completed document is fed into an optical mark reader which scans the document for marks to identify the values selected.

> **Activity**
>
> Describe two applications in which OMR is used.

OMR is often used for multiple choice exam papers. All of the questions and their possible answers will be printed on an answer sheet. The student will indicate the answer to each question by drawing a line through the letter of their choice.

A second application of OMR is the National Lottery. All of the possible selections are organised on a lottery ticket. The player places a line through each of the six numbers selected and the ticket is then entered into an optical mark reader which reads the numbers selected and prints out a receipt.

- *Optical Character Recognition* (*OCR*): this involves the recognition of stylised characters by an OCR reader. The characters are printed using specific fonts which can be recognised by the OCR reader.

Activity

Describe an application in which OCR is used.

OCR is used to read the payment slips on electricity, gas and telephone bills. These bills are known as turnaround documents, as they are produced by computer and part of the document, the payment slip, is detached and returned and used as input to the computer. The payment slip will contain pre-printed information indicating the customer and the amount of the bill.

- *Magnetic Ink Character Recognition* (*MICR*): this involves the recognition by an MICR reader of stylised characters pre-printed in magnetic ink. MICR is used on cheques issued by banks and building societies. The cheque number, branch number and account number are pre-printed in magnetic ink on the bottom of all cheques. When the cheque is passed for clearing, the amount of the cheque is then encoded onto the bottom of the cheque. The cheque is then passed through an MICR reader and its details are stored on disk.

- *Bar Coding*: data is represented as a series of printed bars and spaces which can be read by devices known as scanners. Bar codes are widely used in a variety of industries because they are cheap and reliable and the machines which read the codes are fast, reliable and easy to use. Point-of-sale systems in supermarkets and retail outlets use a scanner to read the bar code. The bar code is then used by the computer to identify the product and its price, which are then displayed. The standard bar code method in Europe is known as EAN (European Article Numbering) and was adopted in 1973. There is currently a demand for more information to be stored in bar codes and for codes to be smaller to fit on items for which the existing bar code is to large. In response to this, two-dimensional codes have been developed such as stacked bar codes. Stacked bar codes are similar to standard bar codes but have a higher data density.

- *Matrix Codes*: these are codes which may replace bar codes by offering a much higher density of data in a smaller area. They represent data using a matrix of light and dark equilateral polygons known as "cells". An example of a matrix code is Data Matrix. Applications of matrix codes are beginning to appear. In the healthcare industry, Data Matrix codes, only a few millimetres in size, are etched by laser onto surgical instruments. The introduction of hand-held readers for matrix codes will increase the adoption of Data Matrix codes by industries such as retail and distribution where there are demands for smaller codes and higher data capacities. A Data Matrix code looks like the following:

- *Smart Cards*: a smart card is a credit card-sized plastic card which has one or more microchips embedded within it. The smart card may be used for a number of different applications for example, paying for telephone calls and for goods and services. The latest development in cashless smart card systems is Mondex which is effectively an electronic purse or wallet. Mondex is intended to be used in place of cash for any transaction at any store which accepts the card.

- *Voice Data Entry (VDE)*: developments are taking place in the area of VDE to enable data to be input directly through speech. There are some obvious problems, such as the wide variety of accents and voice sounds, which make it difficult for a computer to correctly interpret the sound.

Activity

What are the main factors to consider in choosing an input method?

The major factors which should be considered before choosing an input method are:
- the speed at which data needs to be processed;
- the volume of data which needs to be processed;
- the degree of accuracy which is required in capturing the data;
- the cost of the input method against the benefits which will accrue from using it.

2.4 Data Validation

Data validation involves checking that the data which is input to a computer system meets certain criteria.

Both batch systems and on-line systems will have data validation checks incorporated into their processing.

Activity

Identify some data validation checks which could be incorporated into an on-line system.

Data validation in an on-line system could include the following checks:

- *Field Format Check*: for example, a check to ensure that the first character of a person's name is a letter.

    First Name: BRIAN   valid

    First Name: 6RIAN   invalid

- *Field Size Check*: for example, a check to ensure that an account number contains the correct number of characters, say six.

    Account Number: 101033   valid

    Account Number: 10133   invalid

- *Field Range Check*: for example, a check to ensure that the value entered in an employee age field is between 16 and 65.

    Employee Age: 34   valid

    Employee Age: 84   invalid

- *Field Special Value Check*: some fields on a screen may only contain certain values, for example, a marital status field may only contain the values M, D, W or S (married, divorced, widowed or single).

    Marital Status: S   valid

    Marital Status: Z   invalid

- *Field Presence Check*: some fields on a screen must be completed therefore a value must be present. For example, a key field such as account number must always be completed, or perhaps a gender field on a student's record must be completed.

    Gender: M   valid

    Gender: invalid

- *Field Inter-Relationship Check*: to check the compatibility of data entered in more than one field. For example, a title field could be completed with data which is incompatible with data entered in a gender field.

    Title: MISS

    Gender: M   invalid

- *Check Digits*: these are self-checking digits which can be assigned to numeric fields. They are normally appended to key fields in order to detect errors which may occur when the number is transcribed manually. The check digit is generated by the key field itself by applying an algorithm to it. A common use of check digits is in International Standard Book Numbers (ISBNs), which are based on the Modulus-11 algorithm. The following example demonstrates their use:

Q. Calculate the check digit for the ISBN 0 - 9 5 2 0 9 0 4 - 0

ISBN	0	9	5	2	0	9	0	4	0

Step 1:

Apply a weight to each digit in the ISBN. As we are using the Modulus-11 algorithm, set a weight of 10 to the leftmost digit, and reduce the weight by one for each digit to the right:

Weights	10	9	8	7	6	5	4	3	2

Step 2:

Multiply each digit in the ISBN by its weight, and record the products:

Products	0	81	40	14	0	45	0	12	0

Step 3:

Add all of the products together and record their sum:

Sum of products   192

Step 4:

Divide the sum by 11:

Divide by 11   192 ÷ 11 = 17 remainder 5

Step 5:

If the remainder is 0 then the check digit is 0. Otherwise, subtract the remainder from 11 to determine the check digit. If the answer is 10 then the check digit will be X).

Check Digit   11 – 5 = 6

Full ISBN   0-9520904-0-6

A batch system will have a validation program which will be used to validate all of the transactions which have been input to the system, before they are used to update the main data of the system.

Activity

Identify some data validation checks which could be incorporated into a batch system.

A batch system may also have the field checks which have been mentioned above for the on-line system. The following checks will be peculiar to batch systems:

- *Transaction Count Check*: as the transactions are processed they are counted and a record is written to the end of the transaction file which will contain the number of transactions. This record is known as a trailer record. As the validation program reads the transactions it also counts them, and when it reaches the end of the file compares its total against that in the trailer record. Any discrepancies will be printed on an error report. Consider a file of order transactions:

Transaction No.	Customer	Product	Quantity	Price	Total
1	A Kennedy	Twix	3	0.25	0.75
2	R Doyle	Spangles	2	0.20	0.40
3	T Hardy	Wine Gums	5	0.40	2.00
4	W Collins	Chew	55	0.01	0.55
9999	4				

The trailer record contains a transaction no. of 9999 which can be used to identify it as the trailer record, and a count of 4 for the number of transactions on the file.

❏ *Hash Total Check*: a field in each record, which it would normally be meaningless to sum, is used to produce a hash total for the transactions file, and this hash total is also written to the trailer record. For example, consider a number of order transactions containing details of the customer, product, price and quantity of the order. The quantity field could be used to produce a hash total. So, all of the quantities would be summed and written to the trailer record as a hash total. The validation program could then keep its own sum of quantities and compare this to that in the trailer record. Again, any discrepancies will be printed on an error report.

Transaction No.	Customer	Product	Quantity	Price	Total
1	A Kennedy	Twix	3	0.25	0.75
2	R Doyle	Spangles	2	0.20	0.40
3	T Hardy	Wine Gums	5	0.40	2.00
4	W Collins	Chew	55	0.01	0.55
9999	4	65			

Again, the trailer record contains a transaction no. of 9999 which can be used to identify it as the trailer record, and a count of 4 for the number of transactions on the file. On this occasion it also has a hash total of 65 which is the sum of all the quantities.

2.5 Output Devices

The most common output devices are the Visual Display Unit (VDU), often called a *monitor*, and the printer.

❏ *Visual Display Unit (VDU)*: the quality of a VDU is measured in terms of its screen resolution. The higher the resolution, the better the sharpness and clarity of the text or graphics displayed on the VDU. Images are formed on the screen through the use of tiny dots of light known as *pixels*. Each screen is composed of a number of rows and columns of pixels, and the more pixels then the higher the screen resolution. For example, a resolution of 1600 x 1200 indicates 1600 columns x 1200 rows of pixels.

The combination of a VDU and keyboard connected to a mainframe or minicomputer is known as a *terminal*. A microcomputer may also be connected to a mainframe or minicomputer in which case the microcomputer may be referred to as an *intelligent terminal*.

A *touch screen* is a variation of the standard VDU, which can be used as an input device. The user touches the screen to select the required option.

There are many different types of printers available. They are usually classified as:

❏ Character printers, which print one character at a time. Print speeds are expressed as cps (characters per second).

❏ Line printers, which print one line at a time. Print speeds are expressed as lpm (lines per minute).

❏ Page printers, which print one page at a time. Print speeds are expressed as ppm (pages per minute).

The following are the main types of printers available:

- *Dot Matrix Printers*: these are cheap printers with low running costs which operate by striking a ribbon against paper. They can be set for different qualities of print, draft, near letter quality (nlq) and letter quality (lq). They can operate at speeds up to 150 cps for letter quality print. Dot matrix printers are useful for high volume text work such as payslips, invoices etc., but are not suitable for graphics work or high quality printing.

- *Inkjet Printers*: these use a bubblejet technology that heats the ink briefly to boiling and then squirts out an ultra-fine droplet onto the page. They offer high quality printing but at relatively low speeds. A HP Deskjet offers a speed of 3ppm, while a Canon Bubblejet can offer speeds of up to 300 cps.

- *Laser Printers*: these work in a similar way to photocopiers by using a laser imaging system. A laser beam is directed to sweep a dot of light over a drum made of light sensitive material. When the light touches the drum it becomes electrically charged, and the electrically charged drum then attracts the toner and places it on the paper as it passes. Laser printers offer a very good print quality, and fast print speed (18ppm).

Activity

What are the factors to consider in choosing a printer?

The main factors to consider before choosing a printer are:

- the volume of output to be produced;
- the initial cost of the printer;
- the running costs of the printer in terms of the costs of paper, ink cartridges, toner etc.;
- the quality of printing which is required.

An alternative form of output to those above is *speech output*, which is used in a few specialist applications. A current problem with speech output is that it tends to sound unnatural, but developments continue to be made in this area. Multi-media software is now available which can read text back to the user.

2.6 Data Storage Devices

The unit of data storage is a *byte*.

1 Byte = 1 Character

Data storage capacities are normally expressed in megabytes (MB) where:

1 MB = 1,024,000 Bytes

All of the programs and data used within a computer system should be stored on some storage medium which allows it to be rapidly transferred to the CPU whenever

This form of storage is often referred to as *backing storage* or *secondary storage*, as opposed to the main store (memory) within the CPU. The main backing storage media are:

❐ *Magnetic Disk*, which includes both a magnetic disk pack and floppy disk.

❐ *Magnetic Tape*, which maybe in the form of a reel of tape or a tape cartridge, which is similar to a cassette.

❐ *Optical Disk* (CD).

Magnetic tape has been replaced by magnetic disk as the main secondary storage medium. However, as it much cheaper than magnetic disk, it is still used as a means of backing up copies of data held on magnetic disk. Magnetic tape cartridges have storage capacities of up to 5000 MB. The disadvantages of magnetic tape are that it is a *sequential* storage medium and is therefore relatively slow. A sequential storage medium is one on which the data can only be accessed sequentially. This means that to obtain a specific record, the tape must be read sequentially from the beginning until the required record is located.

A magnetic disk is similar in shape and size to an LP record. It is made of metal and its surfaces are coated with a magnetic material. Each surface is composed of a number of concentric tracks, which are divided into a number of sectors.

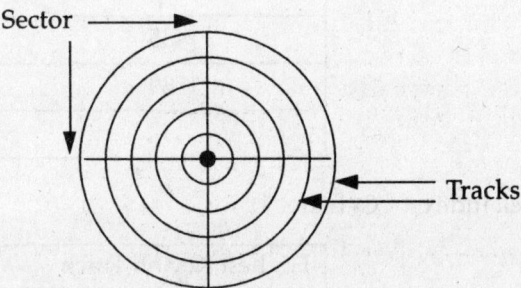

Magnetic Disk (view from above)

A magnetic disk pack is composed of either 6 or 11 single magnetic disks. The inner surfaces of the pack are used to store data, while the two outer surface are merely protective. The tracks immediately above each other in the pack form a cylinder, so if there are 200 tracks on each disk then there will be 200 cylinders in the disk pack. A number of read-write heads are used to store and retrieve the data. The read-write heads are located on the end of arms which move them into position over the required track.

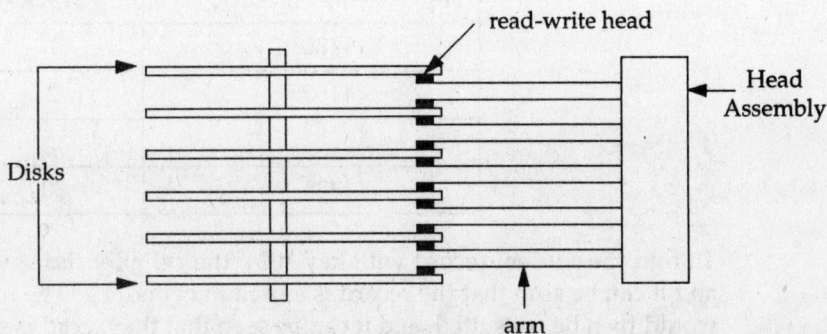

Magnetic Disk pack (side view)

The storage capacity of disk packs has increased significantly in recent years, and storage capacities of 500 MB are now available.

Magnetic disk has the advantage that data can be accessed directly without searching. It is useful to think of direct access in terms of placing a needle on the required track of an LP record, it is not necessary to go through every previous track to get to the one required. This is achieved by each record on the disk being allocated a specific address in terms of the cylinder and track on which it is located. The address of each record is stored in an index, which is looked up to determine the address of the required record, and the read-write heads are then moved to that address. The main types of file organisation on magnetic disk are:

❒ *Indexed Sequential*, in which the records are stored sequentially and an index is maintained of the address of each record. Records can therefore be accessed either sequentially or directly. For example, consider the following example in which student records are stored on magnetic disk. Each student record has a key field, of Student Number, which uniquely identifies the record. Indexes are set up to show the highest key stored on each cylinder and on each track within each cylinder.

Cylinder Index:

Highest Key on Cylinder	Cylinder
1123	1
1435	2
1789	3
...	...

Track Index for Cylinder 1:

Highest Key on Track	Track
1012	1
1029	2
...	...
1123	30

Track Index for Cylinder 2:

Highest Key on Track	Track
1136	1
1163	2
...	...
1435	30

To find the student record with key 1024, the cylinder index would be consulted first and it can be seen that the record is stored in cylinder 1. The track index for cylinder 1 would then be consulted, and it can be seen that the record is stored in track 2, as 1024 is less than 1029.

☐ *Random*, in which the records are stored in random order and an index is maintained to allow them to be accessed directly.

A floppy disk is a small single magnetic disk, which is also organised into tracks and sectors. Floppy disks are useful for backing up copies of data held on the computer's hard disk, and for transferring data between different computers. They have storage capacities of up to 4 MB.

Optical disks (CDs) work on exactly the same principal as a music CD player. A problem with optical disks has been that the data could not be erased and the disks were therefore not rewritable. However, rewritable optical disks are now available. Optical disks store much more data than floppy disks, with storage capacities of over 1000 MB. They are commonly used for storing reference works such as encyclopaedias. Microsoft Encarta contains 28 volumes of encyclopaedias on one CD.

2.7 *Telecommunications and Networks*

A telecommunications system is one which links a number of geographically separate computers or terminals via telecommunications devices. A telecommunications system will perform the following function:

☐ It will transmit data between a number of different computers or between a computer and a number of terminals.

In order to do this a *protocol* is used which allows the sender of the data to communicate with the receiver of the data.

In most cases, terminals will transmit data to a computer, at a different location, via telephone lines. In order to achieve this, the digital signals from the terminal must be converted to analogue form for transmission along the telephone line. It must then be converted back to digital form to be received by the computer. The device used to convert digital signals to analogue, and analogue signals to digital is a *modem*. A modem can plug directly into a normal telephone socket. Increasingly, telephone equipment is becoming digital and eventually modems will become redundant.

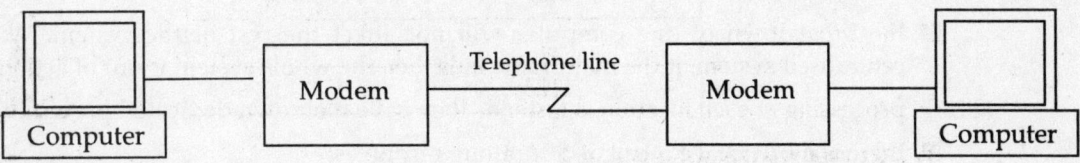

A *multiplexor* is a device which is used to send data from a number of different sources down the same line at the same time.

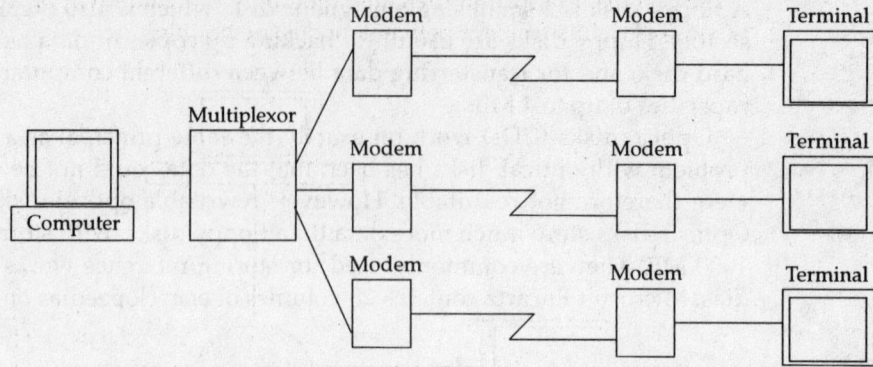

The main data transmission media are:

- *Telephone Lines*: offer comparatively low data transmission rates.
- *Coaxial Cable*: similar to that used for connecting the aerial of a television, offer high transmission rates and high performance.
- *Fibre Optic*: has very high transmission rates, very high performance and very high reliability.

Computers and other devices such as printers and terminals can be connected together to form a network. A *distributed system* is a special form of network in which processing can be carried out at different locations, and data can be distributed among the different locations. Instead of an organisation relying on a mainframe computer with a number of terminals connected, distributed processing allows for a number of minicomputers and microcomputers to be connected at various locations. A distributed system allows the users to have their own processors at each location and therefore removes their dependency on one central mainframe computer. The advantages of a distributed system over a centralised mainframe system are:

- the breakdown of one computer will not affect the rest of the system. With a centralised system, if the mainframe fails then the whole system is out of action;
- processing at each location is faster as they have their own dedicated processor;
- there is more local control of computing resources;
- the cost of minicomputers and microcomputers is significantly lower than that of a mainframe computer.

However, distributed systems depend largely on high quality telecommunications for their success.

The most common type of network, and distributed system, is a Local Area Network (LAN), in which computers and devices are connected together within a room, or a building. The purpose of a LAN is to enable resources such as printers, databases and software to be shared between the users of the LAN. The LAN is managed by special network software such as Novell Netware or Microsoft Windows-NT. Usually, Ethernet coaxial cable is used to connect the computers and other physical resources of a LAN. Most LANs will have a 'file server' which will serve the rest of the network, by offering a hard disk which can be shared by all of the devices connected to the network. There are three main types of LAN topology:

- *Star Network*, in which the nodes, microcomputers and/or terminals are connected to a central main computer. The star topology gives better reliability than the other types mentioned below, as each node is individually connected to the central point. If there is a failure in the cable then only one node will be affected. However, the rates for data transfer between nodes are not high.

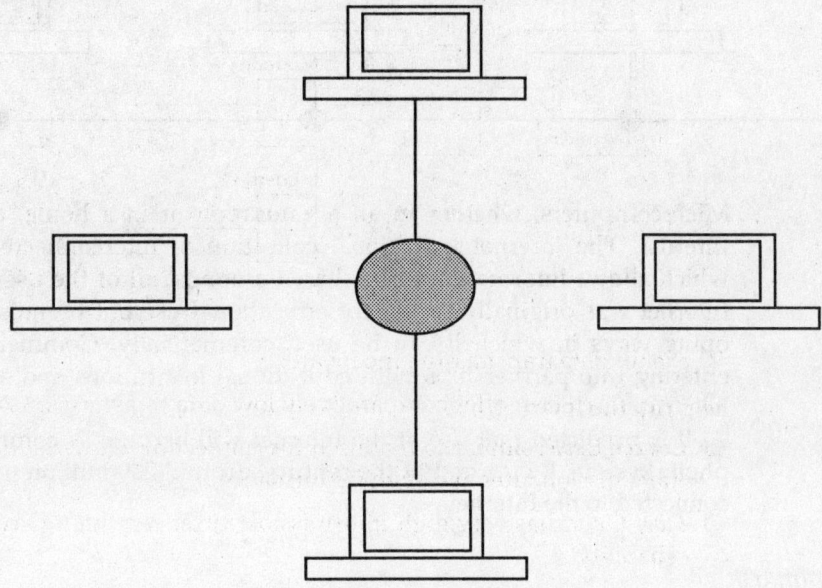

- *Ring Network*, in which the nodes of the network, microcomputers, terminals and file server, are connected in a ring. Data is passed around the ring to its destination. An advantage of the ring structure is that any damage to the cable connecting the nodes can be easily identified.

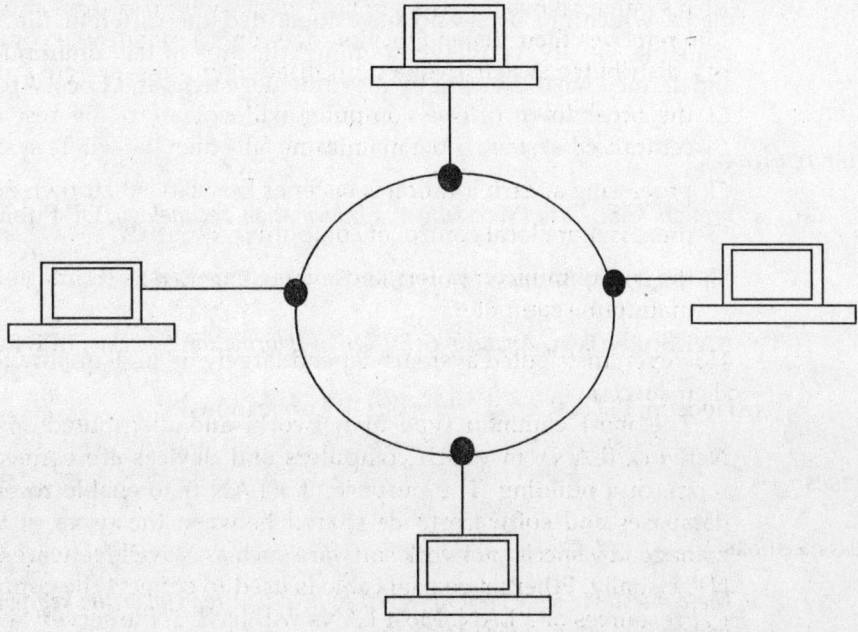

☐ *Bus Network,* in which all of the nodes are connected to a single communication channel. The advantage of the bus structure is the simplicity of the layout and the ease of connecting nodes to the network.

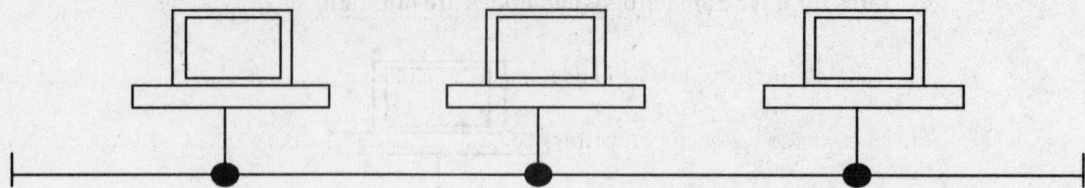

Microcomputers, whether in an organisation or in a home, can gain access to the Internet. The Internet is a global collection of interconnected computer networks which allows information to be shared amongst all of the users of the network. The Internet was originally set up for educational use but organisations are now developing ways in which it can be used commercially. Commercial organisations are entering into partnerships with educational institutions and are providing funds to help run the Internet.

It is predicted that use of the Internet will become as common as use of the telephone system. By the end of the century, around 200 million users are expected to be connected to the Internet.

2.8 Summary

In this chapter we have looked in some detail at the elements which make up a computer system. You have seen the architecture of a computer and the devices of which it is comprised. You have examined the various methods and devices which are available for data capture. You have then identified the main types of data validation which occur in both on-line and batch systems. You have examined the different types of output device which are available. You have looked at the different backing storage media which are used and have identified the different file organisation methods available. Finally, you have examined the area of telecommunications and networks, and defined what is meant by distributed systems and Local Area Networks.

Further reading

French, C.S., *Data Processing and Information Technology*, DP Publications

Clifton, H.D., *Business Information Systems*, Prentice Hall

AAT Study Text, *Analysis & Design of Information Systems*, BPP Publishing Ltd.

Hodson, P, *Local Area Networks*, DP Publications

Exercises

Progress questions

These questions have been designed to help you remember the key points in this chapter. The answers are given at the back of the book.

Complete the following sentences:

1. Hardware is ....
2. Software is ....
3. The elements of the CPU are ....
4. The three types of computer are ....
5. OMR is used in ....
6. The classes of printer are ....
7. The main backing storage media are ....
8. The Control Unit performs the arithmetic and logical operations of the computer.

   True ☐ False ☐
9. MS-DOS is an example of applications software.

   True ☐ False ☐
10. OCR is used by the banking industry for cheque processing.

    True ☐ False ☐

Review questions

These questions have been designed to help you check your comprehension of the key points in this chapter. You may wish to look further than the text in this chapter to answer them fully. You can check your answers by referring to the appropriate section.

11. Explain the main reasons why microcomputers have been so successful. (Section 2.2)

12. Explain what is meant by 'data validation'. (Section 2.4)

13. Explain the differences between Dot Matrix, Inkjet and Laser printers. (Section 2.5)

14. Explain what is meant by 'Indexed Sequential Storage'. (Section 2.5)

15. Explain what is meant by 'Local Area Network'. (Section 2.6)

Multiple choice questions

The answers to these questions will be given in the Lecturer's Supplement.

16. With multiprogramming:
    a) each program is broken down into a number of segments
    b) use of the CPU is shared among the users of the system
    c) many programs share a computer's resources at the same time
    d) a number of CPUs are used at the same time

17. The records addresses in an index will be composed of
    a) the sector on the disk
    b) the cylinder on the disk
    c) the cylinder, sector and track on the disk
    d) the cylinder and track on the disk

18. A multiplexor is used to:
    a) convert digital signals to analogue signals
    b) allow the sender and receiver of data to talk to each other
    c) send data from a number of different sources down the same line
    d) is a type of coaxial cable used in networks

Practice questions

A marking guide to these questions will be given in the Lecturer's Supplement.

19. Describe the differences between a mainframe, a minicomputer and a microcomputer.

20. Explain, with examples, the benefits of automated data capture.

21. Determine the Modulus-11 check digit of ISBN, 1 - 85805 - 027.

22. Describe the differences between magnetic tape and magnetic disk as a backing storage media.

Questions for advanced students

A marking guide to these questions will be given in the Lecturer's Supplement.

23. Describe the different types of Local Area Network available.

24. Explain the advantages and disadvantages of distributed systems.

Assignment

The GoForIT Training Company is a small training company which specialises in the delivery of IT training to organisations and individuals. It employs a number of full-time and part-time staff, and offers approximately 50 courses in various aspects of IT. The majority of courses are scheduled at least three months in advance, but some may be offered at short notice. Courses can either be delivered at GoForIT's premises are at a customer's premises.

Due to problems with the mainly manual system which GoForIT uses to administer and control its business, GoForIT now wishes to install a computer system, running on a Local Area Network, on which to record details of its business including courses offered, courses booked, customers and employees. You have been employed as an IT Consultant by the company and your brief is to recommend the hardware and software which the company will need to purchase for this computer system. GoForIT have stated that the budget for the computer system will not exceed £30,000.

You should consider the following in making your recommendations:

i. the specification of all hardware devices;

ii. details of the communications devices needed to install the LAN;

iii. the operating system software and network software which should be used;

iv. the applications software which will best meet their requirements.

You should produce a report which clearly, and in detail, describes and justifies your recommendations. Also, your report should outline the alternative solutions which were considered.

3 File Systems and Database Systems

3.1 Introduction

This chapter presents an overview of the main concepts involved in the design and use of databases. On completion of this chapter you should be able to:

- understand the basic concepts of databases;
- explain the advantages which a database has over a traditional file system;
- describe the functions of a database management system (DBMS);
- develop an Entity-Relationship Diagram;
- understand and perform the main stages in the normalisation process;
- understand how SQL is used to build and manipulate the physical database.

3.2 The Traditional File System

Before the advent of databases, organisation's stored their computer data in computerised file systems, which are now referred to as traditional file systems. Within a traditional file system, data is organised into a number of files, each of which contains a collection of records. Each record is composed of a number of fields which refer to the basic facts being stored. This hierarchical data organisation is shown below.

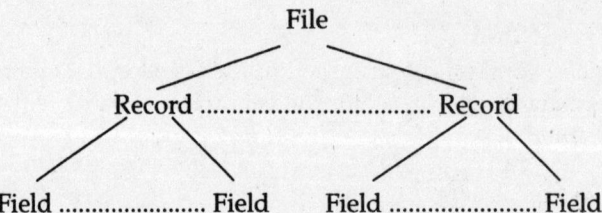

For example, an employee file would contain one record for each employee, with fields such as employee number, name, address, job title etc.

	File Name	Employee File		
Fields	Employee Number	Name	Address	Job Title
Record 1	10201	Alan Icing	12 Stony Lane, Birmingham	Manager
Record 2	10202	Elaine Inch	27 Dukes Road, Birmingham	Supervisor

In order to uniquely identify the records in a file, one of the fields will be designated as a primary key field. In the above example, the key field would be Employee Number, as this will be unique for each employee.

There are a number of different types of file which are used in traditional file systems. The main types are master files and transaction files. Master files contain all of the core data about some area of the organisation. For example, banks would have an Account Master File in which would be stored all of the data about customer accounts. Transaction files are used to update master files, and contain all of the data relating to the transactions over a certain time period, usually one day. For example, a bank's Account Transaction File would record all of the transactions made against customer accounts during one day's business. At the end of day, each record on the Account Transaction File would be read in sequence, and using the Account Number as the key field to the Account Master File, the balance on the Account Master File record would be updated so that it would be correct for the next day's business.

For example, consider the following as the contents of an Account Master File at the beginning of day 1, and the Account Transaction File as showing all of the transactions which took place during day 1.

Account Master File

Account Number	Account Name	Balance
1000001	B White	£100.00
1000002	O Redding	£900.00
1000003	S Cooke	£1000.00

Account Transaction File

Account Number	Transaction Type	Amount
1000003	Credit	£20.00
1000002	Debit	£200.00
1000001	Credit	£50.00
1000003	Credit	£50.00

At the end of day 1, the transaction file is processed against the master file so that all of the balances are correct for the beginning of day 2. After processing, the master file would contain:

Account Master File

Account Number	Account Name	Balance
1000001	B White	£150.00
1000002	O Redding	£700.00
1000003	S Cooke	£1070.00

There are many problems associated with the use of traditional file systems which have lead to their replacement by database systems. Some of the major problems have arisen because each department in an organisation will usually have its own information system and consequently its own files. This means that although much of the data may be common to the entire organisation, each department will have its own version of it. The most significant problems caused by this are:

- unnecessary duplication of data (data redundancy), as each department will just create the files it needs without considering whether the same data is already stored on another file in another department;

❐ inconsistency of data, where the same data can occur on many files and hold different values on each.

For example, consider an organisation which has Ordering and Stock Control departments. Each of these departments will need to know details such as the stock code and stock description of each item in stock. If each of these departments has their own file systems then stock codes and stock descriptions will be held in different files in two separate systems. This creates an unnecessary duplication of data, and increases the possibility of inconsistent data.

> *Activity*
>
> Given the above situation, identify examples of how duplicated data and inconsistent data might arise using the fields stock code and stock description.

The unnecessary duplication of data can be demonstrated by showing that the master files in both the ordering and stock control departments will hold the stock description field.

Ordering Department

Order Master File

Order No.	Order Date	Stock Code	Stock Description	Quantity
10001	11/5/95	A02	486 DX PC	1
10002	11/5/95	A01	386 DX PC	2

Stock Control Department

Stock Master File

Stock Code	Item Description	Quantity in Stock	Reorder Level	Reorder Number
A01	386 DX PC	333	100	300
A02	486 DX PC	76	50	50

If it is assumed that the Stock Control department is responsible for the allocation of stock codes and stock descriptions to items of stock, then they are also responsible for communicating any new, updated or deleted stock codes and stock descriptions to the Ordering department. If Stock Control decide to change the stock description of one item of stock then they need to notify the Ordering department of this change so that all new orders refer to the correct description. If this is not done then inconsistent data will occur as the same stock code will have different descriptions in different departments. For example, if the Stock Control department update the description of stock code A02, and do not communicate this to the Ordering department then the following may occur:

Stock Master File

Stock Code	Item Description	Quantity in Stock	Reorder Level	Reorder Number
A01	386 DX PC	333	100	300
A02	486 SX PC	76	50	50

Order Master File

Order No.	Order Date	Stock Code	Description	Quantity
10001	11/5/95	A02	486 DX PC	1
10002	11/5/95	A01	386 DX PC	2
10003	12/5/95	A03	386 SX PC	3
10004	12/5/95	A02	486 DX PC	5

Although the description of stock code A02 has changed, new orders, in this case 10004 are still being processed with the old stock description.

3.3 Database Concepts

A database can be defined as an organised collection of data which can be accessed by many users and used for many purposes. There are three types of database:

- ❐ Hierarchical Database
- ❐ Network Database
- ❐ Relational Database

Relational databases are the most widely used by organisations of all sizes to store data. They offer simplicity of understanding for users and processing power. Many individuals also use relational database packages, such as Microsoft Access, on personal computers, as a means of storing and organising information relating to their personal affairs. The remainder of this text refers only to Relational Databases.

Activity

Identify three everyday activities which bring you into contact with a database system.

1. The college or university at which you are a student will probably store all of its records about students, attendances and courses on a database system.

2. When you purchase goods in a shop or supermarket, a scanner may be used to read a bar code, and this scanned code is then used to look up the item and price details on a database.

3. A hotel may store all of the information about its rooms and reservations on a database, so that when you attempt to book a room the database will be consulted to see which rooms are available on the dates you require, and updated to show that the room has been reserved if you confirm the booking.

All access to the data on a database is controlled by a software package called the Database Management System (DBMS). The main functions performed by the DBMS are:

- storing the data on disk;
- retrieving the data from disk;
- allowing users and programs to have access to the data;
- maintaining the security of the data;
- providing language facilities for the creation and manipulation of databases.

In a manual filing system the equivalent of the DBMS would be the person in charge of the filing system. For example, they would ensure that the information is stored correctly, they would retrieve files from the filing cabinet when requested, they would store new information, and they would ensure that no one obtains unauthorised access to the filing cabinet. As shown in the diagram below, the DBMS acts as an interface between the database and the programs and users which use the database.

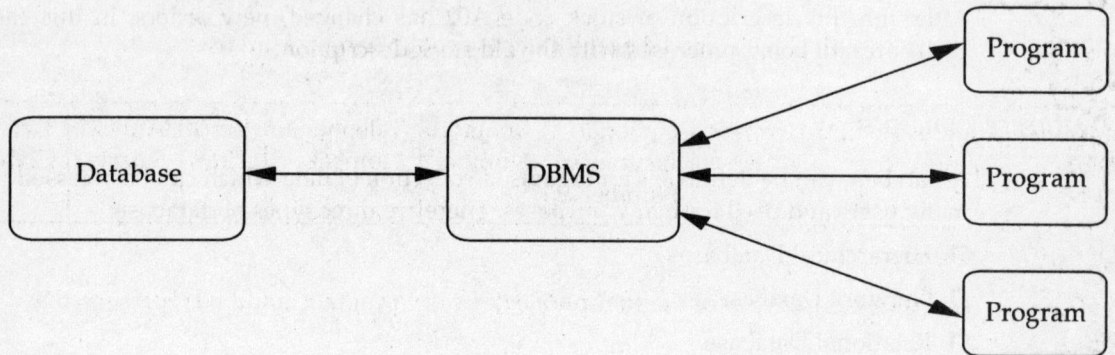

Databases attempt to meet the information needs of the whole of an organisation, not just one area or department. In order to achieve this, the structure of database systems has to be very different from that of file systems. The structure of database systems includes the following:

- Logical Model
- External Views

The logical model is a design of the database which defines the entire structure of the database, and contains a description of all of the data to be stored. As a database may be used by many users from different departments, the logical model must reflect all of their information needs. The most commonly used type of logical model is the Entity-Relationship Diagram which is described in detail in section 3.5.

Because many programs may wish to use different parts of the database, database systems were designed to include external views. An external view defines the part of the logical model which is required by a specific application program. Each program may only have access to the data which is specified in its external view. For example, a program which wishes to calculate the average salary of employees in an organisation would only need to have access to an annual salary field, and this will effectively constitute its external view of the database. This is much more secure than file systems in which the same program would probably need access to the Employee Master File and, would therefore have access to all of the fields on that file.

3 File Systems and Database Systems

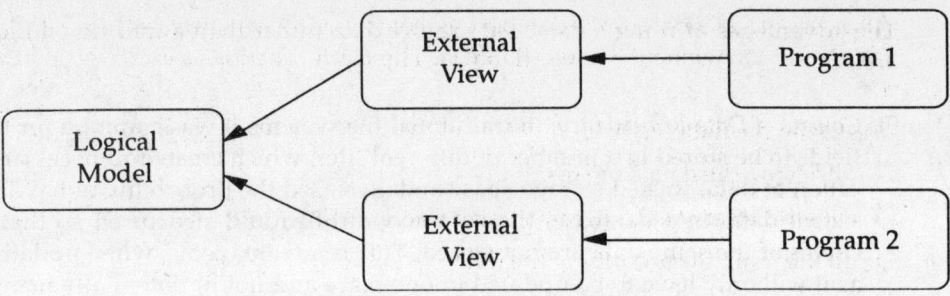

Activity

An organisation's database contains the fields employee number, employee name, department, national insurance number, room number, telephone number, job title, annual salary, tax code. Which fields would you find in an external view for a program which produces a staff phone directory.

In this case the logical model of the database could be represented as:

Employee Number	Employee Name	Department	National Insurance Number	Room Number	Telephone Number	Job Title	Annual Salary	Tax Code

and the external view of the staff phone directory program could be represented as:

Employee Name	Department	Room Number	Telephone Number

The fields contained in the external view of the staff phone directory program would be employee name, department, room number and telephone number. The remaining fields would still be on the database but could not be accessed as they are not specified in the external view. The use of external views can protect data from unauthorised access and potential corruption.

3.4 Advantages of Databases

There are many advantages which a database system has over a traditional file system.

Activity

Considering the content of the previous two sections, what do you think are the main advantages which a database system has over a traditional file system.

The advantages of using a database to store data rather than a traditional file system are:

- *Control of Data Redundancy*: in traditional file systems it was common for the same fields to be stored in a number of different files, which created unnecessary duplication of data, wasted storage space and increased the probability of having inconsistent data. In a database, the data is controlled and structured so that several copies of the same data are not stored. This is advantageous when updating data, as it will only have to be updated in one place and not in potentially many places as on a traditional file system.

- *Data Independence*: in a traditional file system, when a new field is added to a file, each program which uses that file, irrespective of whether they need the new field, will have to be changed. In a database system, when a new data item is added to the logical model, only those programs which need the new data item in their external view will have to change. Therefore the data which is held on a database is said to be independent of the programs which are used to access it.

- *Data Standards*: in a traditional file system each department can set up its own files using whatever data it requires without having to conform to any standards with regard to the naming and format of fields. In a database system, the most important role is that of the Database Administrator (DBA). The DBA is responsible for the design, management and operation of the database, and will define and enforce standards for the representation of the data in the database. Anyone in an organisation who requires access to existing data, or requires the creation of new data will need to go through the DBA.

- *Data Security*: in a traditional file system all of the data on all of the files is available to anyone who wants it. If someone requires access to only a few of the fields on a file there is no way of giving them access to the file and restricting that access to only those fields. This could lead to the corruption of data. A database is protected from unauthorised access as programs may only access the data specified in their external views. The DBMS will also have various security procedures such as passwords installed which add further to data security.

- *Future Systems Development*: database systems are designed to take into account the future requirements of an organisation. This has the advantage that if a new application is to be developed it is likely that all of the data which the application requires is already stored on the database, and so the cost and time of the development can be significantly reduced. In a traditional file system, even if all of the data was held on the system, it is likely that it will be held on many different files and therefore complicated processing may be necessary to copy the required data onto specific application files.

- *Systems Maintenance*: the cost, time and effort required in the maintenance of database systems is significantly lower than that for traditional file systems. Traditional file systems do not offer data independence, therefore programmers will often be engaged in amending many programs because the structure of one file has changed. This type of programming is unproductive, as the programmers carrying it out are therefore not available to effect any program changes required by users. In database systems the amount of unproductive programming is much lower than in file systems.

3.5 The Entity-Relationship Diagram

The Entity-Relationship (E-R) Diagram is a design of the database which represents all of the information requirements of a system. As with all designs, there may be many possible solutions to the design of an E-R Diagram, some better than others, but none necessarily either right or wrong. The DBA is responsible for the design of the E-R Diagram, working in collaboration with systems analysts and users. The components of the E-R Diagram are:

❑ *Entity*: an entity is something of interest to the organisation about which information needs to be stored. It can be a physical object such as a person or product, an event such as a lecture, or an intangible object such as a course. An entity will eventually be a table in the physical database. When naming entities, names which are meaningful to the user should be chosen, and the singular should always be used. In an E-R Model entities are represented as rectangles:

❑ *Relationship*: a relationship can be defined as the association between two entities. There are, in fact, two relationships between each two related entities. For example:

    CUSTOMER places ORDER   the relationship name is 'places'
    CUSTOMER books ROOM   the relationship name is 'books'

There are three types of relationships which are:

❑ one-to-one (1:1)   e.g. One Man married to One Woman

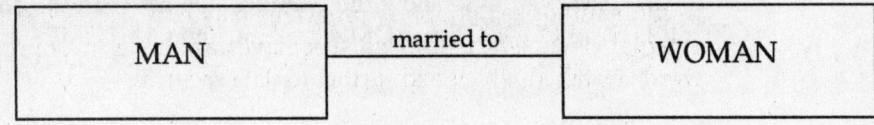

❑ one-to-many (1:m)   e.g. One Team contains Many Players

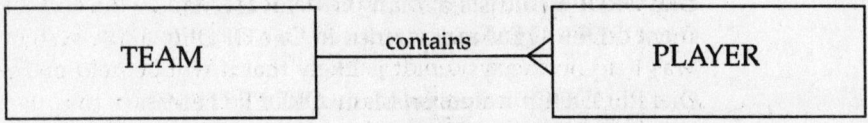

❑ many-to-many (m:n)   e.g. Many Lecturers teach Many Courses

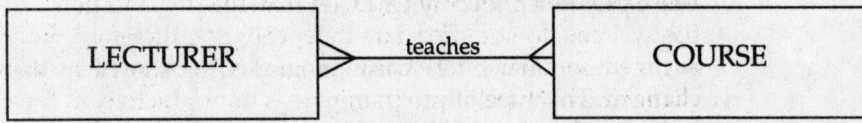

❑ *Attribute*: the term attribute is used to refer to a fact or an item of information which needs to be stored about an entity. It is an alternative name for a field, but is usually used only in the context of the logical database. Examples of attributes of

the Lecturer entity may be Lecturer Number, Lecturer Name, Lecturer Address, Lecturer Birth Date and Lecturer Salary.

Each entity will have a key identified, which may consist of one or more attributes. The key will uniquely identify each entity. The key of the lecturer entity above would be the attribute Lecturer Number as this will be unique for each lecturer.

In order to create the relationship between two entities, the key of one of the entities must be used as a foreign key in the other entity. Consider the following:

Entity	Attributes
PLAYER	Player Name (Key), Player Address, Date Of Birth
TEAM	Team Name (Key), Home Ground, Manager

The relationship between these entities is:

TEAM contains PLAYERS(1:m)

In order for the relationships between PLAYER and TEAM to be created the Team Name attribute would be used as a foreign key on the PLAYER entity. Therefore PLAYER would contain the attributes:

Player Name (Key), Player Address, Date Of Birth, Team Name (Foreign Key)

The foreign key will always be the key attribute from the entity on the one side of a one-to-many relationship. In the above case, the team entity is on the one side, therefore its key will act as a foreign key in the player entity.

Activity

Create an E-R Diagram to show the relationships between the entities ORDER and ORDER ITEM, PRODUCT and ORDER ITEM, and CUSTOMER and ORDER.

Given the above information, the following relationships can be identified:

One ORDER consists of Many ORDER ITEMs
One ORDER ITEM is contained in One ORDER

One PRODUCT occurs on Many ORDER ITEMS
One ORDER ITEM refers to One PRODUCT

One CUSTOMER places Many ORDERs
One ORDER is placed by One CUSTOMER

Only the one-to-many relationships need to be shown in the E-R Diagram, which would be drawn as follows:

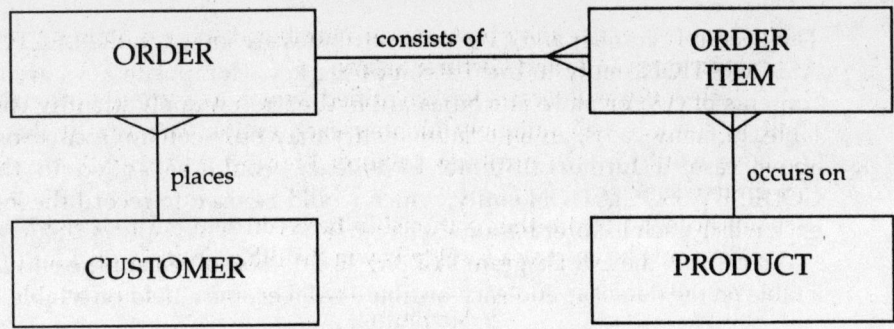

An E-R Diagram must be refined to remove any one-to-one and many-to-many relationships. The entities in a one-to-one relationship should be merged if they share many of the same attributes. For example, if two entities EMPLOYEE and MANAGER were identified with the relationship:

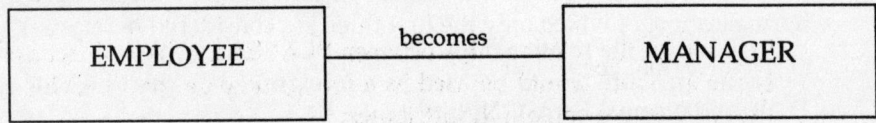

Then if these entities shared the majority of attributes, the entities would be merged into one entity, EMPLOYEE.

All many-to-many relationship should be refined as they cannot be implemented efficiently in relational databases. If we consider the many-to-many relationship between LECTURER and COURSE:

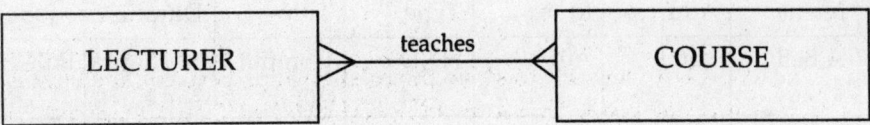

A third entity, known as an associative entity is always introduced between the two entities of a many-to-many relationship. In this case it will give:

The attributes including keys and foreign keys will be something like:

Entity	Attributes
LECTURER	Lecturer Number (Key), Name, Address, Job Title
LECTURER COURSE ASSOCIATION	Lecturer Number, Course Id (Composite Key)
COURSE	Course Id (Key), Description, Duration

The Lecturer Number and Course Id attributes are joined in the LECTURER COURSE ASSOCIATION entity to form a composite key. Composite keys are used when the contents of two or more attributes are needed to uniquely identify each record on a table. In many cases, an associative entity may only contain a composite key. In the above case, a further attribute, Experience, could be added to the LECTURER COURSE ASSOCIATION entity, which would be used to record the length of experience which each lecturer has on each course.

To convert the E-R Diagram to a physical database, each of the entities will become a table on the database and each attribute will become a field on a table.

3.6 Normalisation

In the design of a logical model for a database there will be many possible designs which the DBA can consider. In order to decide upon the most effective design the DBA may use a technique known as normalisation. Normalisation aims to improve the logical design by making it free of redundant data and flexible enough to permit the future addition of entities, attributes and relationships. There are five levels of normalisation, of which only the first three are considered here:

- First Normal Form (1NF);
- Second Normal Form (2NF);
- Third Normal Form (3NF).

Whenever the tables in a logical design have undergone the normalisation process they are said to be normalised. To demonstrate 1NF, 2NF and 3NF we will apply the rules for each to the following set of unnormalised data on students and courses.

Student_ Number	Student_ Name	Student_ Address	Course_ Id	Course_ Type	Course_ Title	Course_ Duration	Course_ Mode	Grade
001	A Bell	London	A01	HND	Computing	120 hours	Full-Time	MERIT
001	A Bell	London	B02	RSA	French	20 hours	Part-Time	PASS
002	B Careful	Croydon	C01	HNC	Business Studies	80 hours	Part-Time	DISTINCTION
002	B Careful	Croydon	B01	RSA	Italian	20 hours	Part-Time	MERIT
003	G Upshot	Ealing	A02	HND	Business	120 hours	Full-Time	PASS

In order to perform normalisation it is necessary to begin by converting the tables to 1NF, and, when that is completed proceed to 2NF and then to 3NF.

- *First Normal Form (1NF)*: the aim of 1NF is to remove all of the repeated occurrences of attributes in the logical design, and therefore ensure that the final physical database will be free of redundant data. In order to convert the above into 1NF it will be necessary to remove the repeated data and place it into a separate table.

Activity

Convert the above data into first normal form.

Examination of the data reveals that the attributes Student_Number, Student_Name and Student_Address are repeated unnecessarily. In order to achieve 1NF, these attributes should be placed in a separate table, which will be called the Student Table. The remaining attributes will be placed in a Course Table.

Student Table

Student_Number	Student_Name	Student_Address
001	A Bell	London
002	B Careful	Croydon
003	G Upshot	Ealing

Course Table

Course_Id	Course_Type	Course_Title	Course_Duration	Course_Mode	Grade
A01	HND	Computing	120 hours	Full Time	MERIT
B02	RSA	French	20 hours	Part Time	PASS
C01	HNC	Business Studies	80 hours	Part Time	DISTINCTION
B01	RSA	Italian	20 hours	Part Time	MERIT
A02	HND	Business	120 hours	Full Time	PASS

❑ *Second Normal Form (2NF)*: to be in second normal form the table must already be in 1NF, and all of the non-key attributes must be dependent on the key attribute. To demonstrate what is meant by dependence, consider only the Student Table. Each student will have only one student number, but it is possible for more than one student to share the same name and, possibly, the same address. Therefore the attribute Student_Number can be used to identify the name and address of one student. But, neither the Student_Name attribute nor the Student_Address attribute necessarily identify only one student number. Therefore, the attributes Student_Name and Student_Address are dependent upon the Student_Number. In this case Student_Name and Student_Address are the non-key attributes and Student_Number is the key attribute.

In order to convert to 2NF, any attribute which is not dependent on a key attribute must be removed and placed in a different table along with the key attribute on which it is dependent. The Student table above is already in 2NF as it is obvious that both the attributes Student_Name and Student_Address are dependent upon the key attribute Student_Number. Therefore, only the Course Table has to be normalised into 2NF.

Activity

Convert the Course table into second normal form.

In the Course table the key attribute is Course_Id. Each non-key attribute is then checked to determine if it is dependent upon Course_Id. This check reveals that only the following attributes are dependent upon Course_Id:

- Course_Type because each course can only be of one type, but there may be many courses of that type. For example, there are many different HND courses.

- Course_Title because each course can only have one title, but there may be many courses with the same title. For example, there may be many courses with the title Business Studies.

- Course_Duration because each course has only one duration, but many courses may have the same duration. For example, there may be many courses which last two years, such as HND and A' Level.

The other attribute, Grade, is not dependent on Course_Id as a grade is awarded for a particular student on a particular course. Therefore, the attribute Grade is dependent on the Course_Id and the Student_Number combined. Course_Id, Student_Number and Grade must therefore be placed in a separate table, with Course_Id and Student_Number as a composite key.

After normalising into 2NF, the following tables are created:

Course Table

Course_Id	Course_Type	Course_Title	Course_Duration	Course_Mode
A01	HND	Computing	120 hours	Full-Time
B02	RSA	French	20 hours	Part-Time
C01	HNC	Business Studies	80 hours	Part-Time
B01	RSA	Italian	20 hours	Part-Time
A02	HND	Business	120 hours	Full-Time

Class Table

Course_Id	Student_Number	Grade
A01	001	MERIT
B02	001	PASS
C01	002	DISTINCTION
B01	002	MERIT
A02	003	PASS

- *Third Normal Form (3NF)*: to be in 3NF the table must already be in 2NF, and any non-key attribute which is dependent upon some other non-key attribute, should be removed and put into a new table. Again, we only need to consider the Course table, as, examination of the Student and Class tables show that there are no non-key attributes which are dependent upon any other non-key attributes.

> *Activity*
>
> Convert the above Course table into third normal form.

In the Course table, the attributes Course_Duration and Course_Mode are dependent upon the non-key attribute Course_Type. This is because all HND courses are full-time and 120 hours, all HNC courses are part-time and 80 hours, and all RSA courses are part-time and 20 hours. After normalising into 3NF, the following tables result:

Course Table

Course_Id	Course_Title
A01	Computing
B02	French
C01	Business Studies
B01	Italian
A02	Business

Course_Definition Table

Course_Type	Course_Duration	Course_Mode
HND	120 hours	Full-Time
RSA	20 hours	Part-Time
HNC	80 hours	Part-Time

Once each stage of the normalisation process is completed, the tables are said to be fully normalised.

3.7 Building the Physical Database

The initial physical database will be built directly from the logical model. It will then be fine tuned to most efficiently meet the performance requirements of the system. With most DBMS packages, Structured Query Language (SQL) is used to build the database, insert data into the database and manipulate the database. Each DBMS will have its own version of SQL, although there are currently moves to define international standards for SQL. The version used in this chapter is for the Oracle relational DBMS.

A physical relational database is easily defined using the SQL (Structured Query Language) commands of:

- ❏ CREATE TABLE to create the base tables for the database. For example, the Course table could be created by the command:

```
CREATE TABLE COURSE
    (COURSE_ID          CHAR(3)             NOT NULL,
     COURSE_TITLE       CHAR(16)            NOT NULL,
     COURSE_TYPE        CHAR(3)             NOT NULL,
     PRIMARY KEY        (COURSE_ID)
     FOREIGN KEY        (COURSE_TYPE));
```

The value CHAR represents the type of data which will be stored in the field. The value NULL means that a value is not present in the field. The fields in the Course table are set to NOT NULL to indicate that values must always be entered. The field COURSE_ID is specified as the primary key for the table. The field COURSE_TYPE is specified as a foreign key, as it is the primary key of the Course_Definition table. The specification of a foreign key creates referential integrity between the Course and Course_Definition tables. This means that a course type must exist on the Course_Definition table before an individual course can be specified to be of that type. Also, the record in the Course_Definition table which specifies a particular course type cannot be deleted while there are records in the Course table which refer to that course type.

The Course_Definition table would be created by:

```
CREATE TABLE COURSE_DEFINITION
    (COURSE_TYPE        CHAR(3)             NOT NULL,
     COURSE_DURATION    CHAR(9)             NOT NULL,
     COURSE_MODE        CHAR(9)             NOT NULL,
     PRIMARY KEY        (COURSE_TYPE));
```

- CREATE INDEX to create indexes via which the data on the database can be accessed more quickly. For example, a unique index could be created on the course table using the primary key field:

CREATE UNIQUE INDEX CIDX ON COURSE (COURSE_ID);

The UNIQUE specifies that each course will have its own COURSE_ID, and duplicates will not be allowed. The index name is CIDX. The user can choose any index name that they wish, however, it is a convention to include an 'X' in the index name.

Activity

Write the SQL commands to create the Student table and Class table. Also, create a unique index on the primary key field of the Student table.

The Student table will be created using the following SQL statement:

```
CREATE TABLE STUDENT
    (STUDENT_NUMBER     SMALLINT            NOT NULL,
     STUDENT_NAME       CHAR(10)            NOT NULL,
     STUDENT_ADDRESS    CHAR(10)            NOT NULL,
     PRIMARY KEY        (STUDENT_NUMBER));
```

The SQL statement which creates a unique index on the key field is:

CREATE UNIQUE INDEX SNUMX ON STUDENT (STUDENT_NUMBER);

The Class table will be created using the following SQL statement:

```
CREATE TABLE CLASS
    (COURSE_ID          CHAR(3)       NOT NULL,
     STUDENT_NUMBER     SMALLINT      NOT NULL,
     GRADE              CHAR(11),
     PRIMARY KEY        (COURSE_ID, STUDENT_NUMBER));
```

The field GRADE may contain null values as when the record is first created the students will not yet have been allocated any grades for any courses. The primary key in this instance is a composite key of the fields COURSE_ID and STUDENT_NUMBER.

The INSERT statement is used to add data to a table. For example, to add a record to the Course table:

```
INSERT INTO COURSE
(COURSE_ID, COURSE_TITLE, COURSE_TYPE)
    VALUES ('A01', 'Computing', 'HND');
```

> *Activity*
>
> Write the SQL statements to insert data into the Course_Definition, Student and Class tables.

The statements are:

i. INSERT INTO COURSE_DEFINITION
    (COURSE_TYPE, COURSE_DURATION, COURSE_MODE)
        VALUES ('HND', '120 hours', 'Full-Time');

The student number field is of type SMALLINT therefore the value which is inserted for this field does not have to be enclosed by apostrophes.

ii. INSERT INTO STUDENT
    (STUDENT_NUMBER, STUDENT_NAME, STUDENT_ADDRESS)
        VALUES (001, 'A Bell', 'London');

iii. INSERT INTO CLASS
    (COURSE_ID, STUDENT_NUMBER, GRADE)
        VALUES ('A01', 001, 'MERIT');

The basic SQL command for manipulating the database, in order to retrieve data, is the SELECT command which has the basic format:

```
SELECT  field(s)
    FROM            table(s)
    WHERE           condition(s);
```

The WHERE clause is optional, but the SELECT and FROM clauses are mandatory.

The SQL statement to retrieve the course id and course title of all courses on the Course table can be written as:

SELECT   COURSE_ID, COURSE_TITLE
   FROM COURSE;

or more simply as:

SELECT *
FROM COURSE;

where * is used to represent all fields on the table.

> *Activity*
>
> Write the SQL command to retrieve the student number, name and address of all students living in London.

Assuming that the address field will only contain the town or city, then the SQL statement is:

SELECT   STUDENT_NUMBER, STUDENT_NAME, STUDENT_ADDRESS
   FROM STUDENT
   WHERE STUDENT_ADDRESS = 'London";

This is only a very brief introduction into SQL. Much more complicated SELECT statements can be written which use functions, conditional statements, additional clauses etc.

3.8 Summary

In this chapter we have examined both traditional file systems and database systems. You have identified the main components of database systems and the advantages which they have over traditional file systems. You have seen the functions of the Database Management System (DBMS) and the role played by the Database Administrator (DBA). You have examined the development of Entity-Relationship Models and how they provide a design for the database. You have interpreted and applied the rules of normalisation to produce normalised tables and a more flexible design for a relational database. Finally, you have seen how SQL can be used to build and manipulate the database.

Further reading

Ricardo, Catherine, Database Systems, Macmillan

Howe, D.R., Data Analysis For Data Base Design, Edward Arnold

Van Der Lans, Rick, The SQL Guide to Oracle, Addison-Wesley

3 File Systems and Database Systems

Exercises

Progress questions

These questions have been designed to help you remember the key points in this chapter. The answers are given at the back of the book.

Complete the following sentences:

1. The main types of file in a traditional file system are ....

2. A database is..

3. A Database Management System controls...

4. The Database Administrator is responsible for..

5. A logical data model is..

6. External views are used to..

7. An entity is...

8. Hierarchical databases are the most popular type of database.

    True ☐ False ☐

9. Storage and retrieval of data is performed by the Database Administrator.

    True ☐ False ☐

10. The E-R Diagram should be refined to remove one-to-many relationships.

    True ☐ False ☐

Review questions

These questions have been designed to help you check your comprehension of the key points in this chapter. You may wish to look further than the text in this chapter to answer them fully. You can check your answers by referring to the appropriate section.

11. Explain some of the problems with the use of traditional file systems. (Section 3.2)

12. Describe the advantages of using a database system. (Section 3.4)

13. What are the main components of an Entity-Relationship Diagram. (Section 3.5)

14. What are the aims of the normalisation process. (Section 3.6)

Multiple choice questions

The answers to these questions will be given in the Lecturer's Supplement.

15. Which of the following is not a function of a Database Management System:
    a) to ensure that all users can access all of the data in the database
    b) to control access to the database

c) to provide security for the database
d) to assist with the design of a logical model

16. Which of the following are acceptable examples of entities:
    a) Product Code
    b) Employee Salary
    c) Account Transaction
    d) Account

17. When a many-to-many relationship is refined:
    a) two one-to-one relationships are created
    b) a one-to-one relationship and a one-to-many relationship are created
    c) two one-to-many relationships are created
    d) many-to-many relationships should not be refined

18. One-to-one relationships should be refined when:
    a) most of the attributes on each entity are different
    b) most of the attributes on each entity are the same
    c) one-to-one relationships should not be refined
    d) none of the above

19. The aims of first normal form are:
    a) to remove attributes which are not dependent on the key
    b) to remove repeating groups of attributes
    c) to include attributes which are dependent on the key
    d) none of the above

Practice questions

A marking guide to these questions will be given in the Lecturer's Supplement.

20. Explain how a database system reduces data redundancy and offers data independence.

21. Explain the advantages of using a logical model and external views in database systems.

22. Explain how Entity-Relationship Diagrams are used in the development of databases.

Questions for advanced students

A marking guide to these questions will be given in the Lecturer's Supplement.

23. Design an E-R Diagram for the following situation. A hospital specialises in the treatment of diseases and in operations. Patients admitted to the hospital may be treated for diseases, and/or may undergo one or more operations. While in hospital, patients will remain in one of the hospital's wards. Operations may be either emergency or planned, and each operation is performed by one of the hospital's surgeons. For planned operations, the surgeon is arranged in advance.

24. Normalise the following into 1NF, 2NF and 3NF.

Employee _Number	Employee _Name	Salary	Employee _Manager	Employee_ Department	Hours	Project_ Name	Project_ Manager	Estimated _Time
A001	N Abbot	£15,000	S Gurning	Order Control	35	Foreign Orders	A Woodman	200 Hours
A001	N Abbot	£15,000	S Gurning	Order Control	15	Order Matching	B French	40 Hours
A002	G Gollum	£21,000	S Gurning	Order Control	25	Foreign Orders	A Woodman	200 Hours
A002	G Gollum	£21,000	S Gurning	Order Control	70	Order Systems	Z Mooney	1000 Hours
A003	H Oboken	£19,000	P Mire	Management Services	35	Foreign Orders	A Woodman	200 Hours
A003	H Oboken	£19,000	P Mire	Management Services	50	Order Systems	Z Mooney	1000 Hours
A003	H Oboken	£19,000	P Mire	Management Services	35	Sales Processing	R Mc Donald	100 Hours

Assignment

The Getwellsoon Hospital specialises in the treatment of diseases. It has twenty wards and one operating theatre. The wards are categorised as general, pre-op, post-op and isolation. There are 12 general wards each with 16 beds, 1 pre-op ward with 4 beds, 2 post-op wards each with 8 beds and 5 isolation wards with 1bed each. Each ward is identified by its block and room number. All patients admitted to the hospital are assigned to a particular ward. However, during their stay they may be transferred to different wards.

Patients may be admitted for the treatment of one or more diseases. Treatment may require surgery, in which case an operation is scheduled. All operations will be classified as either scheduled or emergency, and will be performed by one or more surgeons. Surgeons will be assigned to scheduled operations in advance. The hospital keeps records of each disease which it treats, including the symptoms of the disease and the recommended treatment.

Patients are referred to the hospital by their GP. They are then diagnosed, and if necessary admitted immediately or arrangements are made for future admission. Patients are sent notification of scheduled admissions one week in advance, and a bed is reserved in the appropriate ward for their arrival.

The hospital calls all patients back for a check-up one month after they have been discharged from the hospital. If a patient is transferred to another hospital, then all records concerning the patient are also transferred.

i. Identify all of the entities in the above, and describe the attributes which will be required for each entity. You can use whatever attributes you feel are necessary.

ii. Draw an Entity-Relationship Diagram, showing all of the entities and the relationships between them.

iii. Perform the normalisation process, up to and including 3NF, upon all of the attributes which you have identified.

iv. Write the SQL statements to build all of the tables which you have identified. Include the primary and foreign keys for each table.

v. Write the SQL statements to insert data into each of the tables which you have created.

4 Developing Information Systems

4.1 Introduction

This chapter presents an overview of the main stages involved in the development of information systems. On completion of this chapter you should be able to:

- identify the main roles in systems development;
- identify the main stages in the development of a computer system;
- describe the main areas of a feasibility study;
- describe the process of systems analysis;
- describe the process of systems design;
- explain the main tasks involved in the implementation of a computer system;
- describe how prototyping is used as an alternative systems development methodology.

4.2 Roles in Systems Development

The *Systems Analyst* will analyse, design, test and implement the system. The qualities which a systems analyst should possess are:

- the ability to understand possibly complex areas of the business;
- a good technical knowledge of the main areas of computing;
- the ability to communicate effectively with users and members of the project team;
- the ability to understand a problem and to logically provide a solution.

The *Programmer* will produce the computer programs which actually realise the new system. Programmers must be logical thinking, thorough, have the ability to work at a very detailed level and have good technical skills.

The *Database Administrator (DBA)* will be responsible for the design and implementation of the database for the new system. The DBA will be supported by the *Database Administration Team*.

The *Data Processing (DP) Manager* is responsible for all of the work undertaken by the systems department of an organisation. Their primary duties are to plan, contol and co-ordinate the activities of the systems department.

The *Project Manager* will, in conjunction with the *Project Management Team*, be responsible for the day-to-day high-level management of all aspects of the development. The Project Manager will report to the Project Steering Group on progress, and will place requests for future project resources.

The *Project Steering Group* will include senior management from the user department and the DP Manager. Its responsibilities are:

- to monitor and control the project in terms of cost, efficiency and progress;
- to appoint senior staff to manage the project;
- to give approval for each stage of the project to proceed.

> *Activity*
>
> Consider a project to develop a computer-based information system which will encompass two business areas of a large organisation. Draw a hieracrchy chart to show the involvement of the above roles in the project.

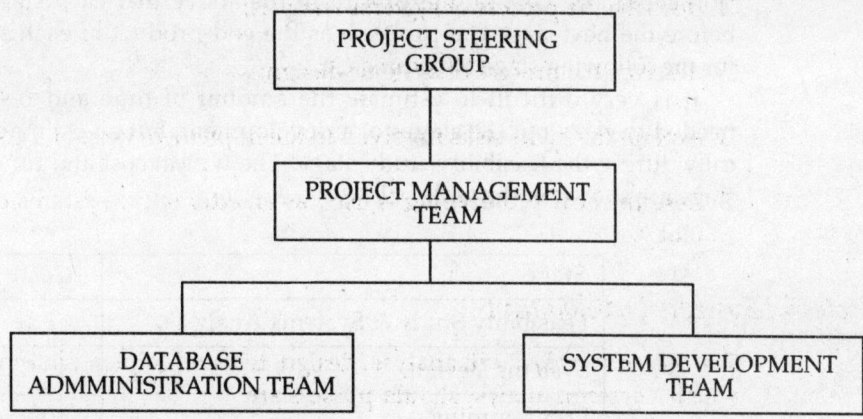

The System Development Team will contain systems analysts and programmers. The number of analysts and programmers will vary depending on the stage in the development. The System Development Team may be sub-divided into a number of smaller teams, each dealing with a specific business area of the development.

4.3 The Systems Development Life Cycle

The phrase "systems development" covers the development of computer systems from the initial idea through to the eventual installation of a working system. The development of any particular system is carried out by a project team which will generally consist of users, managers and Data Processing (DP) staff. The DP staff involved will be systems analysts, programmers and database analysts. All projects to develop information systems go through a number of stages known collectively as the Systems Development Life Cycle (SDLC). Each stage in the SDLC is distinct and consists of a number of activities which must be performed, by the project team, in order for the stage to be completed successfully. For each stage, a number of end-products or deliverables are identified which must be produced by the project team. In order for the stage to terminate successfully the end-products must be approved and signed off by the Project Steering Group.

We are now in a position to identify the stages of the SDLC, and their respective end-products:

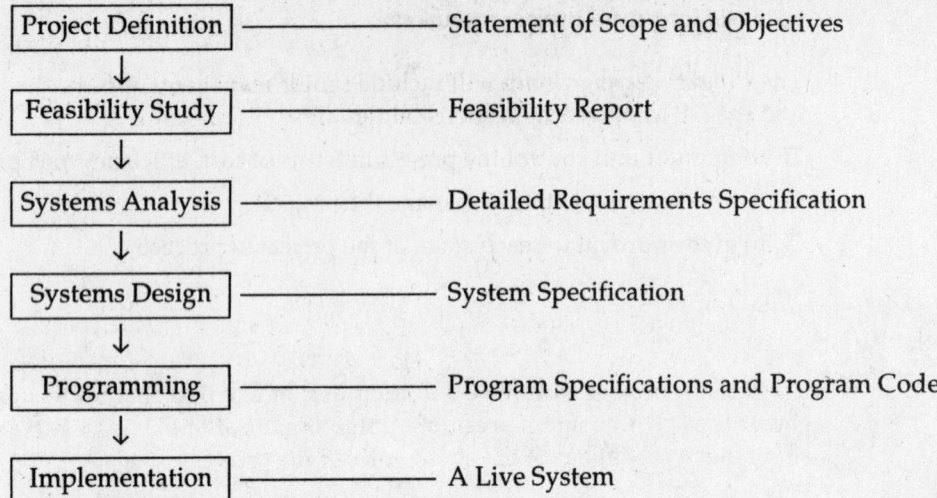

You should be able to interpret from the above that each stage must be completed before the next stage can proceed, as the end-product of each stage is a pre-requisite for the following stage to commence.

It is very difficult to estimate the amount of time and resources which will be needed to carry out the stages of a development, but an estimate must be made, typically during the feasibility study stage. The typical cost and time percentages for each stage are shown in the table below.

Stage	Cost	Time
Feasibility Study & Systems Analysis	3%	10%
Systems Design	18%	25%
Programming	40%	35%
Implementation & Maintenance	39%	30%

System Development Cost & Time Estimates

The SDLC is an example of a systems development methodology. A methodology is simply a collection of stages, procedures and techniques to assist systems developers in the construction of new information systems. They were introduced to attempt to rectify the major weaknesses of early systems developments such as:

❏ information systems were inflexible in that much time and effort was needed to make alterations;

❏ the quality of the completed system was less than initially desired;

❏ users did not participate in the development of information systems;

❏ documentation was of a poor standard;

❏ planning of the development was difficult and often haphazard.

Methodologies attempt to bring a structured approach to the development of information systems by explicitly stating the tasks which have to be performed at each stage of the life cycle. Essentially, methodologies provide a framework for the development. There are a number of methodologies which are widely used such as SSADM (Structured Systems Analysis and Design Method), and IE (Information Engineering). Each methodology has an underlying philosophy and approaches the task of systems development in its own way. The terminology, rules and activities assigned to each stage may differ from one methodology to another. Some may combine Project Definition and Feasibility Study in a single stage, others may group design and programming in a single stage. In what ever way a methodology approaches system development, the basic sequence of development activities will remain the same.

The most widely used methodology in the UK is SSADM which covers the following stages of the life cycle:

- Feasibility
- Systems Analysis
- Systems Design

SSADM is often used in conjunction with other methods such as strategic planning and structured programming to cover the complete life cycle.

The objectives of all methodologies include the following:

- to produce better quality and flexible systems;

- to enable good communication between DP staff and users;

- to be supported by computer-based tools to facilitate the recording and documentation of the stages of the process;

- to provide improved project planning and control;

- to assist users to contribute to the development process.

This is an appropriate point to mention CASE (Computer-Aided System Engineering) tools and their use with methodologies. The purpose of CASE tools is to automate the techniques used in the development of information systems. A CASE tool will usually consist of the following components:

- a diagramming component to support the diagrams, required during analysis and design, that analysts previously drew using pen and paper;

- a data dictionary component for all of the data relating to the system.

Some CASE tools may also have Screen and Report Generators to provide the user with control over the screen and report output, and some may have Code Generators to produce the programs required by the system.

Many methodologies have CASE tools associated which effectively automate all of the techniques used in the methodology. An example is the Information Engineering Facility (IEF) which is used with the Information Engineering methodology. Some CASE tools may be designed to be flexible enough to work with a number of different methodologies. The use of CASE tools usually means that more time will be spent on the analysis and design stages of a project than on the programming stage. This is especially true if the CASE tool incorporates a Code Generator.

4.4 Project Definition and Feasibility Study

The project definition stage is mainly concerned with analysing the organisation at a strategic level and defining the information systems which are needed in order for the organisation to meet its aims and objectives. Some reasons for initiating a systems development might be:

- to meet new requirements of the business;
- to solve problems in an area where a system is not functioning effectively.

The objectives and scope of the new information system will be defined along with estimates as to its duration, cost and complexity. These must be agreed with senior management of the organisation before the feasibility study can commence.

The feasibility study is conducted to determine whether or not a project should proceed before any major expenditure is undertaken. The study should address the following:

- the problems with the existing system;
- the objectives of the proposed system;
- evaluation of a number of options for a new system and the recommendation of one for development.

Activity

A Project Steering Group will specify the terms of reference for a feasibility study, specify some items which a terms of reference might include.

If you specified any of the following then you are on the right lines:

- an overview of the current system;
- performance criteria for the new system;
- the benefits which the new system will bring;
- a recommendation for the new system;
- a plan for developing the new system;
- time scales for the development;
- the skills required to carry out the development;
- a budget for the cost of developing and running the new system.

As the feasibility study is so important to the eventual success of the system development, it will be conducted by highly experienced and senior DP staff in conjunction with senior representatives from the user community.

Activity

Identify some benefits which a new system might bring to a business.

Hopefully you identified some of the following:

- savings in staff costs;
- savings in operating costs;
- increase in sales revenue;
- greater customer satisfaction;
- improved information for more effective decision-making.

It should be remembered that most of the costs of the project will be incurred during the development and before any benefits are noticed or gained. Some cost/benefit analysis needs to be undertaken in order to evaluate the benefits against the cost in achieving them.

The final step of the feasibility study stage is to produce the Feasibility Study Report which should include:

- a definition of the current situation;
- an outline of various possible solutions;
- the reasons for choosing the preferred solution including a cost/benefit analysis;
- a specification of the preferred solution including its technical and operational implications.

The feasibility report will have to be approved and "signed-off" by the Project Steering Group before detailed systems analysis can begin.

4.5 Systems Analysis

The systems analysis stage is carried out by systems analysts working in close co-operation with users. As mentioned previously, the principal objective of this stage is for the analyst to produce a detailed specification of the business requirements for the new system. In order to achieve this objective the systems analyst must perform a number of tasks which fall into the following categories:

- understand the current system;
- identify the user's requirements for the new system;
- interpret the user's requirements for the new system;
- define the user's requirements for the new system.

Activity

Suppose you are a systems analyst employed to carry out the systems analysis for a proposed new system. Your initial brief is to understand the business area for which the new system is intended, describe your initial approach towards accomplishing this task.

Systems analysts are rarely experts in the business area in which they are required to work, however they must at least have a working understanding of the business area. For a systems analyst assigned to develop an information system in an unfamiliar business area, a first step towards acquiring this understanding would be to read around the subject area using journals, text books and other reference materials. As the majority of information gathering during the analysis stage will involve some form of interaction between the analyst and the user, it is important that the analyst is able to communicate effectively with the user about the business. For example, the analyst should be able to understand and use the relevant business terminology. The success of a project can depend, in part, on the nature of the working relationship between the DP staff and the users. The establishment of a professional working relationship will be enhanced, if the users believe that the DP staff have a sufficient understanding of the underlying business area to effectively build an information system which meets the requirements of the business.

> *Activity*
>
> Identify the main information gathering methods which you would adopt and some advantages and disadvantages of each.

You may have identified the following:

- interview;
- questionnaire;
- observation of the current system in operation;
- analysis of existing documentation.

It is usual that all four methods are used at different times during information gathering.

Interviews are useful for obtaining in-depth information and establishing working relationships with users. They are the most common method of information gathering. The established practices for arranging and conducting interviews should be adhered to. For example, the analyst should arrange the interview well in advance, ensure that the interviewee knows the purpose of the interview, remain polite and objective during the interview, take careful notes during the interview.

Questionnaires can be useful for obtaining small amounts of information from a large body of users. For example, they would be appropriate for obtaining information from geographically widespread users. A disadvantage of questionnaires is that they often receive a slow and poor response.

Observation of the current system allows the user to verify findings obtained through interview and questionnaire, and should also increase the analyst's understanding of the business area. Observation can be costly and time consuming, as it may involve analysts travelling extensively.

Analysis of existing documentation such as input forms and reports is useful in conjunction with the other methods. They can form a useful source from which the analyst can identify the data which needs to be held by the system. The analyst should ask the user for copies of documentation during interviews and observation of the current system.

All of the information gathered during the systems analysis stage will allow the systems analyst to answer two key questions:

1. What needs to be done by the new system?

2. What data does the new system need to hold?

The structured approach to systems analysis focuses on addressing these two questions. In order to answer the first question, the analyst will need to identify the processes that the system will need to perform. A process is defined as a business activity which does at least one of the following:

- produces outputs for the business;
- gathers new information for the business;
- controls the business;
- or involves decision-making within the business.

Examples of processes would be Pay Employee, Check Received Item, Store Received Item and Invoice Customer.

In order to answer the second question, the analyst will need to identify all the things about which the organisation must hold data in order to operate. Something about which data must be held is known as an *entity*. We have dealt with this subject in more detail in the chapter on databases, but at the moment it is sufficient to identify the following as example entities: Employee, Product, Department and Car.

> *Activity*
>
> A college wishes to develop a new Enrolment System to handle the enrolment of students onto its courses. Using your existing knowledge of college enrolment, identify some of the processes which the system will need to perform, and the data which the system will need to hold.

Some of the processes which a College Enrolment System will need to perform will include:

- Interview Candidate
- Make Offer
- Enrol Student
- Transfer Student Between Courses
- Remove Student
- Set Up Course
- Amend Course Details

From the above processes you should identify that there are two entities on which the system will need to hold data, namely Student and Course. The elements of data which will need to be held on each entity are known as attributes. The table below shows some of the possible attributes of the entities Student and Course.

Entity:	Student	Entity:	Course
Attributes:	Student Number Name Address Postcode Phone Number Date Of Birth Next Of Kin	Attributes:	Course Code Course Title Duration Examining Body

Finally, it is important to remember that systems analysis is usually carried out by small teams, consisting of a number of analysts and at least one user from the respective business area. Throughout the analysis stage the analysts and users should have regular review meetings to walkthrough progress on current tasks and eventually with the production of the Requirements Specification. At the end of the analysis stage the users will have to "sign-off" the Requirements Specification therefore they need to play an active and continuous role in its production.

4.6 Systems Design

While systems analysis is concerned with defining what a system should do, in systems design the analysts concentrate on defining how the system will operate. In order to be successful the design phase requires the analyst to have specialist computer expertise and a clear understanding of the business requirements.

> **Activity**
>
> Identify the main areas which a systems analyst must address during systems design.

You may have identified some of the following areas:

Input Form Design: the design of forms which are used to collect the data which will be input to the system. Forms should be designed so that data entry can be completed easily and with as few errors as possible. Form design is important as it represents a link between the user and the system. The area of data collection has potentially detrimental performance implications in terms of the speed and accuracy of data capture. There have been many developments to automate this area of processing such as the use of scanners in shops and supermarkets to read bar codes, and EPOS (Electronic Point Of Sale) devices which can read and check credit cards.

- *Report Design*: all of the reports which the system produces will need to be designed. The analyst, in conjunction with the user, will need to consider the frequency and timing of reports, the contents and the method of producing the reports. Again, it is important that users play a leading role in report design.

- *Screen Design*: screens should be designed so that they are easy to read and complete. Text, graphics and colour should be chosen to enhance the design and due consideration should be given to ergonomic principles.

- *Dialogue Design*: the design of the 'conversation' between the user and the computer system. A number of design features can be built into the dialogue such as appropriate error messages, pull-down menus, highlighting of fields in error, colour coding of screen fields and help lists. Again, the screen and dialogue design are important as they represent the interface or link between the user and the computer system.

- *Database Design*: the data requirements established during the systems analysis stage will continue to be refined until they meet all of the requirements of the system as effectively and efficiently as possible. Once this is completed the actual physical database can be constructed.

☐ *Procedure Design*: all of the activities which the information system will perform need to be designed. The logical steps involved in each will be clearly identified to more easily facilitate the production of program specifications during the Programming stage of the development.

As you can see, the design will describe all of the components of an information system and define the way they fit together into a complete system. As with anything else which requires design, there may be many possible designs for an information system. The design which should be chosen is the one which best meets the user requirements within the time, financial and technical constraints imposed on the system development.

The number of analysts involved in systems design will be significantly larger than the number involved in systems analysis. It is again important that the user plays an active role in design through regular reviews and walkthroughs.

At the end of the system design stage, the details of the design will be documented in a System Specification. The specification acts as the final statement of what the system will do and it must be accepted by the Project Steering Group and other interested parties before work on the construction of the system can begin.

4.7 Programming

During the programming stage, the System Specification is used as the basis for the specification of programs to carry out the processing of the system. A Program Specification will be written for every program in the system, detailing the inputs, processing and outputs required.

> *Activity*
>
> What do you consider to be the main stages in the production of a fully tested program?

The main stages are design, code and test. The most commonly used approach to program design is Structured Programming. With this approach the overall problem is broken down into sub-problems, and each sub-problem is successively refined until it can be easily translated into a programming language. The design produced is often referred to as a program algorithm and generally written in a form of Structured English (pseudocode) . The algorithm will specify the steps which the program must carry out in order to meet the requirements of the program specification. Often, the algorithm will be subject to a walkthrough by a group of other programmers to ensure that it does what it is supposed to do. Coding of the program into a programming language should only begin when the program algorithm is complete. The theory of structured programming is that it should be relatively easy to translate the algorithm into any programming language.

All programs must be thoroughly tested to ensure that they produce the correct results. A test plan must be produced for every program. The test plan should identify the tests to be conducted and the expected results of each test. In any program there may be a number of alternative routes through the program therefore to completely test a program every possible route must be tested. In order to achieve this the programmer will have to set up test data which reflects every possible situation which may arise.

Programming is the first stage in the project in which programmers become actively involved. The number of analysts can be reduced to a level at which they may be outnumbered by programmers. Users must still be kept informed of progress but will adopt a lower profile during programming.

In projects which use structured development methodologies and CASE tools it is common for the program code to be automatically generated from the program algorithm. This has led to a large reduction in the amount of programming effort expended on the programming stage, but increases the importance of complete and thorough analysis and design.

4.8 Implementation

The implementation stage of the life cycle consists of the steps that need to be taken to put the new system into operation. The main steps in implementation are:

- *Hardware and software installation*: the site must be prepared in advance of hardware being installed. Consideration needs to be given to issues such as the environment in which the hardware will be kept, the number of sites, site security and communication links.

- *Staff training*: training should cover all the functions which the new system offers and should take place over a sufficient period of time to allow the users to become familiar with the system. Preferably training should be conducted by the user community and targeted at all system users.

- *System testing and acceptance testing*: system testing should be conducted after all individual programs have been tested. Systems analysts conduct system testing to ensure that the whole system functions correctly. Acceptance testing is carried out by both users and systems analysts and represents the final check that the system meets the requirements.

- *File conversion*: all of the data held on the old system must be converted into the correct format for the new system. Conversion programs are often written to convert the data into the new format.

- *System changeover*: the changeover from the old system to the new system.

> *Activity*
>
> You have been asked by a local sports club to produce a plan for the conversion of a membership file from the manual system to that required by the new computer system. List the main steps which will need to be included in your plan.

The plan should include the following steps:

1. Check all of the manual files and remove all dead records, for example, records of people who are no longer members of the club.

2. Transcribe the data from the source files onto documents to enable the data to be input and checked easily.

3. Identify control totals for the data, for example, a total of the number of member records.

4. Key the data from the completed documents onto a computer file.

5. Print a listing of the computer file and check it against the documents.

6. Check the control totals on the documents and check against those produced by the computer file.

There are four main methods of changeover from an old system to a new system:

- *Direct changeover* is the complete replacement of the old system with the new system on an appointed day. If this approach is adopted then the changeover is best done at a weekend or during a holiday period when there is a break in the normal stream of work. This is a very risky approach as, if the new system has any serious problems, there is nothing to fall back on. Direct changeover requires very careful planning and testing if it is to be successful.

- *Parallel running* is the old system and new system running together for a period of time until everyone is satisfied that the new system functions correctly. The sets of results from each system will be compared and any discrepancies will be reconciled on the new system. This approach is suitable when the changeover is from one type of computer to another, as the data to be processed can be fed into both systems almost concurrently. A disadvantage of parallel running is the degree of duplication of effort involved.

- *Pilot operation* in which the new system is implemented for a limited area of the organisation. When the pilot version is working satisfactorily then it will be implemented throughout the organisation. This approach is suitable where a number of branches have to undergo changeover. The system will be implemented in one branch and then successive branches until it is in all branches.

- *Phased implementation* is the introduction of the new system in a number of phases. One part of the system is implemented and run for a period of time and then a second part and so on. The phases are usually selected by the functions which the system must perform. If a system is phased by functions then the core functions of the business will be covered in the first phase, and successively less important functions in subsequent phases. This approach is adopted when a system is too large to be easily implement in one piece. The project team needs to ensure that the new functions to be implemented successfully interface with the functions of the existing system.

Once implemented, the system must be maintained to deal with:

- new information requirements;
- new processing requirements;
- errors in the system.

Following implementation, the system will need to be maintained by analysts and programmers to ensure that it continues to function correctly. As an information system ages the maintenance costs tend to increase and the system becomes more difficult to maintain. If performance becomes unsatisfactory and the maintenance costs are too high then a case may exist for developing a new system.

In the implementation and maintenance of computer systems, the systems department and the organisation as a whole need to be aware of the regulations of the Data Protection Act and the Computer Misuse Act. The Data Protection Act was passed to protect individuals from the misuse of data held about them on computer systems. For example, if the data is inaccurate or if it is passed to third parties without the individual's consent. The act sets up a register of data users which contails full details of the data which they use and its purposes. The principles of data protection are:

- Data must have been obtained fairly and lawfully.
- Data must only be used for the purposes described in the data user's register entry.
- Data must only be disclosed in accordance with the user's register entry.
- Data must be accurate and up-to-date.
- Data must not be kept for longer than is necessary for the stated purposes.
- Data must be disclosed to the data subject on request.
- Data must be protected against loss or unauthorised disclosure.

The Computer Misuse Act was introduced to counter the widespread misuse of computer systems. The act covers practices such as:

- hacking into a computer system;
- copying computer programs without proper authority;
- placing computer viruses in systems;
- entering false records onto ccomputer files.

4.9 Prototyping

Systems development using the SDLC can be a long and expensive process. Often, projects may take as many as three or four years before they are implemented. During this period it is possible that the requirements which have been specified during systems analysis will have changed and new requirements may have come to light. It may then be very difficult for the new system to react to these new requirements and effectively incorporate them. Due to these problems, alternative methods of developing computer systems have been developed.

One such method is known as prototyping. It involves the building of a prototype of the system and then repeatedly refining the prototype until it fully satisfies the user requirements. The steps involved in protoyping are:

1. Identify the user's basic requirements for the system.

2. Develop a prototype for the system.

3. The user evaluates the prototype to determine how effectively it meets their requirements.

4. Refine the prototype in response to the user's evaluation.

5. Repeat 3 and 4 until the user is fully satisfied that the system meets their requirements.

The major priority with prototyping is to quickly produce a working system which the user can evaluate.

Systems which are developed using the prototyping methodology differ from systems developed using the SDLC in the following respects:

- protyped systems are developed more quickly than SDLC systems;
- protyped systems can more easily repond to changes in requirements;
- the user is more involved in the design of protyped systems;
- prototyped systems require the systems analyst to spend less effort in information gathering;
- many end-user computing tools are suitable for use with prototyping.

However, prototyping is not appropriate for all systems. It is most appropriate for the development of small applications and for Decision Support Systems. The development of large and complex systems should be performed using the SDLC.

Activity

Describe how prototyping could be incorporated into the systems design stage of the SDLC.

One of the main areas of systems design is the design of the interface between the user and the system. Two aspects of this interface are the individual screens which the system will present to the user, and the dialogue which will take place between the user and the system. Prototyping can be effectively used as a methodology for the design of screens and dialogues. A prototype of the screens and dialogues can easily be created. The prototype can then be evaluated by the users and refined as necessary.

4.10 Summary

In this chapter we have looked at the main stages in the development of information systems. You have identified the main roles in systems development. You have seen how the stages form a life cycle for a development project, and you have identified the objectives of system development methodologies. The main considerations in conducting a feasibility study and the benefits which a new system might bring to an organisation have been identified. The approach which the systems analyst must take to the conduct of systems analysis has been defined. You have considered the main elements in system design and you have seen the main steps in programming. You have looked at the various approaches which can be taken to the implementation of a new system. Finally, you have seen how prototyping can be used as an alternative methodology to the SDLC.

Further reading

Ashworth, C & Slater, L, *An Introduction to SSADM*, McGraw-Hill

Weaver, P, *Practical SSADM*, Pitman

Exercises

Progress questions

These questions have been designed to help you remember the key points in this chapter. The answers are given at the back of the book.

Complete the following sentences:

1. A methodology is a collection of ....

2. Systems development methodologies adopt ....

3. The feasibility study determines ....

4. The principal objective of systems analysis is ....

5. Systems analysis concentrates on ....

6. Systems design concentrates on ....

7. The main stages in programming are ....

8. Questionnaires are the most commonly used method for information gathering.

    True ☐ False ☐

9. An algorithm is the designed solution to a programming problem.

    True ☐ False ☐

10. Direct changeover is the least risky implementation strategy.

    True ☐ False ☐

Review questions

These questions have been designed to help you check your comprehension of the key points in this chapter. You may wish to look further than the text in this chapter to answer them fully. You can check your answers by referring to the appropriate section.

11. Explain the benefits of using a methodology in the development of information systems. (Section 4.3)

12. Describe the steps which the analyst must undertake during systems analysis. (Section 4.5)

13. What are the main areas which the analyst must consider during systems design. (Section 4.6)

14. Compare the different implementation strategies and identify the advantages and disadvantages of each method. (Section 4.8)

Multiple choice questions

The answers to these questions will be given in the Lecturer's Supplement.

15. Structured development methodologies focus on:
    a) the processes which a system performs
    b) how the system will operate
    c) the data which the system will need
    d) the technical requirements of the system

16. The terms of reference for a feasibility study will specify:
    a) the technical specification of the new system
    b) all possible solutions for the system
    c) the budget for the cost of developing the system
    d) the number of analysts and programmers needed for the development

17. During systems analysis the systems analyst will:
    a) design the reports needed by the new system
    b) model the information and processes of the new system
    c) produce program specifications
    d) install the hardware for the new system

18. Systems development projects are controlled by:
    a) a team of analysts
    b) a team of analysts and users
    c) a Project Steering Group
    d) the chief executive of the organisation

19. Users should be involved in:
    a) all stages of the development life cycle
    b) the analysis stage only
    c) the feasibility and analysis stages only
    d) the implementation stage only

Practice questions

A marking guide to these questions will be given in the Lecturer's Supplement.

20 Explain what is meant by structured programming.

21 Describe the main steps in system implementation.

22 Explain what is meant by phased implementation.

Questions for advanced students

A marking guide to these questions will be given in the Lecturer's Supplement.

23 Compare and contrast the SSADM and Information Engineering (IE) methodologies. Outline the benefits and possible disadvantages of each approach.

24 Obtain information on CASE tools and describe the benefits of CASE tools to systems development.

Assignment

You have been appointed as Project Manager for the project to develop a computer system for the Getwellsoon Hospital. Using the Getwellsoon Hospital scenario from the previous chapter, do the following:

i. Produce a project plan showing the activities to be performed at each stage of the development and the roles required to perform them.

ii. Describe how you intend to involve users in each stage of the development.

iii. Describe how the prototyping methodology will be used during the design stage of the development.

iv. Produce an implementation plan for the system.

5 Systems Analysis Techniques

5.1 Introduction

This chapter defines the main techniques which are used during systems analysis. On completion of this chapter you should be able to:

- explain the concept and objectives of Process Analysis;
- apply the technique of decomposition to identify the elementary processes within a business area;
- understand the use of Data Flow Diagrams to model systems;
- understand the use of a Data Dictionary as a store of data;
- understand the use of Entity Life Histories to model the changes to the data held in a system;
- understand the use of Decision Tables to clarify complex processing;

5.2 Process Analysis

As described in the previous chapter, during systems analysis the systems analyst is concerned with two main areas:

- *Data Modelling*: which is used to identify the data which the new system will need to hold.

- *Process Analysis*: which is used to identify what needs to be done by the new system.

Data modelling is examined in detail in chapter 3. The objective of process analysis is to identify the business processes which occur in the area under investigation so that they can be incorporated into the new system.

A process is defined as a type of business activity which does at least one of the following:

- A process produces outputs needed inside or outside the business. For example, a sales catalogue which is distributed outside the business, may be produced by a process called Produce Sales Catalogue.

- A process gathers information for the business. For example, details about orders may be recorded by a process called Take Order.

- A process controls areas within the business. For example, the level of stock held in a warehouse may be controlled by a process called Check Stock.

- A process involves decision-making. For example, a decision such as the choice of a particular supplier may be achieved by a process called Choose Supplier.

5 Systems Analysis Techniques

During systems analysis, it is usual for a team of systems analysts to investigate, analyse and produce a requirements specification for an area of the business. Through investigation and analysis, the analysts will identify the processes which occur in the area. Using the technique of decomposition, the analysts will decompose (break down) the area into a number of high-level processes. Each high-level process will then be decomposed, in turn, into its constituent processes. Decomposition will continue until the lowest level of processes, known as *elementary processes*, are identified. This method of decomposition can be represented as follows:

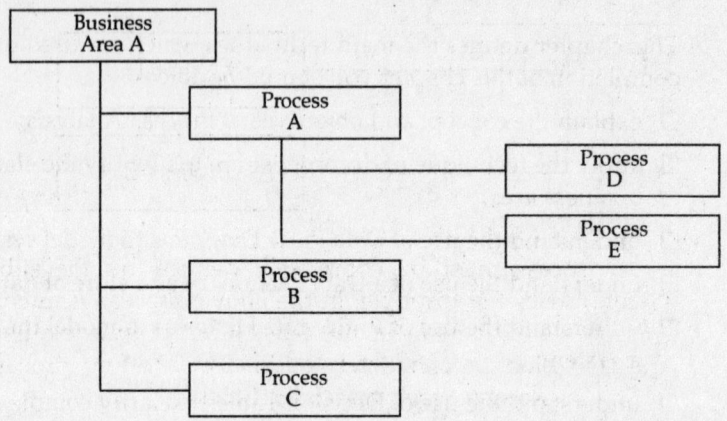

The business area A is composed of three high-level processes, A, B and C. One of these, process A, is itself composed of two further processes, D and E.

Consider a real-life example in which an analyst has to investigate and analyse the stock control area of an organisation. They may identify that this area is composed of two high-level processes one dealing with stock and the other with suppliers. They may then look at each of these areas in turn and identify the processes which occur in each. Their investigations may conclude with the identification of the following processes:

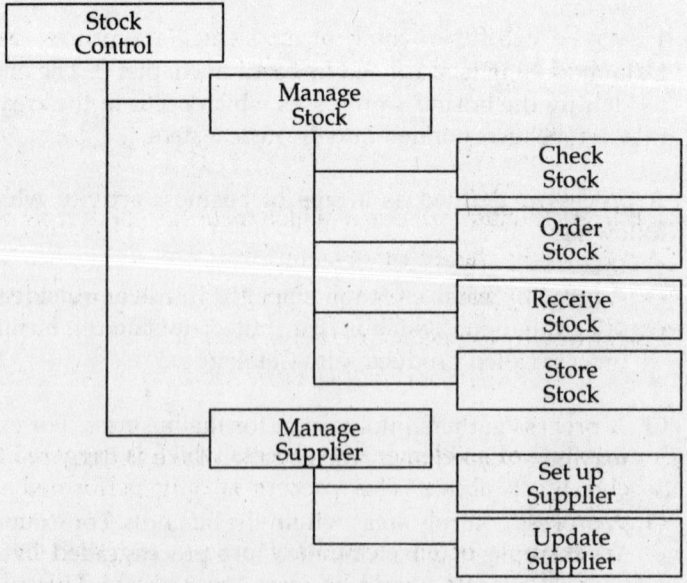

The rules which govern the decomposition of processes are:

i. A process, which is decomposed, must consist of two or more processes.

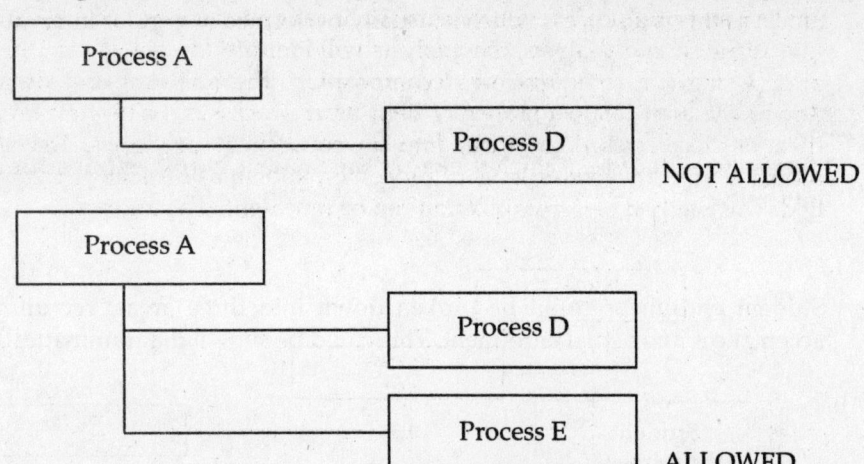

ii. A process must be completely defined by the subprocesses of which it is composed. For example, in the above, process A must be completely defined by processes D and E. In the Stock Control example above, the process 'Manage Stock' must be completely defined by the four processes 'Check Stock', 'Order Stock', 'Receive Stock' and 'Store Stock'.

Decomposition of processes should proceed in a top-down manner, and should cease when the lowest level of processes, known as elementary processes, are reached. An elementary process has the following characteristics:

- it is triggered by the arrival of an input, the completion of another elementary process or by a specific time being reached;
- once started, a process will continue executing until it is complete, without having to wait for any other process or the arrival of other information;
- it has no subprocesses which can be executed independently.

It may be helpful to think of an elementary process as something which can be performed by one person at one time.

Activity

Identify elementary processes which meet each of the following characteristics:
- triggered by the arrival of an input;
- triggered by the completion of another elementary process;
- triggered by a specific time being reached.

An example of an elementary process which is triggered by the arrival of an input is Receive Stock above. This process is only performed when goods arrive from a supplier.

An example of an elementary process triggered by the completion of another elementary process would be Store Stock above. This process can only be executed after the goods have been received and are accepted as valid by the process Receive Stock.

An elementary process which is triggered by a specific time being reached is Check Stock, as this is a process which is usually performed at regular intervals.

> *Activity*
>
> Identify the processes which make up the student enrolment area in a college or university.

Student enrolment could be broken down into three areas, recruitment, handling acceptances and actual enrolment. This could be shown diagrammatically as:

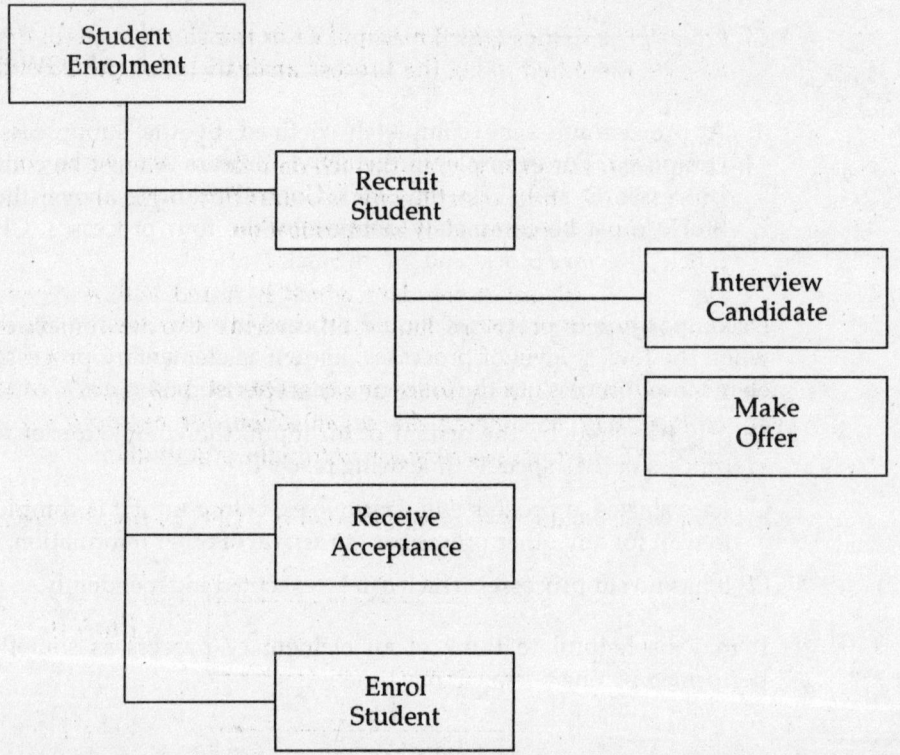

In the above example, Interview Candidate, Make Offer, Receive Acceptance and Enrol Student are all elementary processes as they have no subprocesses.

The rule for naming processes is to use a verb followed by an object. The verb should be as precise as possible, therefore words like record, handle and process should be avoided. The object will be singular and will usually refer to an entity or attribute in the data model. For example, the process Enrol Student will create a new occurrence of the entity Student.

Processes can be found using any of the information gathering methods of user interviews, questionnaires, observation of the current system and analysis of existing documentation.

All of the processes identified by the systems analysts will have to be verified with the users. It is very important that they are as complete as possible, as it is the elementary processes which indicate the processing which the new system will have to perform.

5.3 Data Flow Diagrams (DFD)

The creation of DFDs to model systems is one of the main techniques used during systems analysis. The objectives of DFDs are:

- to represent the flows of data around a system;
- to define the processes that manipulate or transform the data;
- to identify the external sources and external recipients of data;
- to show where data is held within the system;
- to act as a means of communication between the analyst and the user.

The components of a DFD are:

- *Processes*: activities which manipulate or transform the data in a system. Processes may be identified using the process analysis technique described in the previous section.

- *Data Flows*: channels through which data flows between the other components of a DFD. For example, order details is a data flow which comes from a customer into the ordering department of an organisation.

- *Data Stores*: identifies the data which is stored within a system. For example, a college system will store data on all students who have enrolled.

- *External Entities*: the sources or recipients of data outside of the system. External entities may be outside the organisation, for example a customer, or may be another department or function within the organisation.

Each of these components is represented in a DFD by the following symbols:

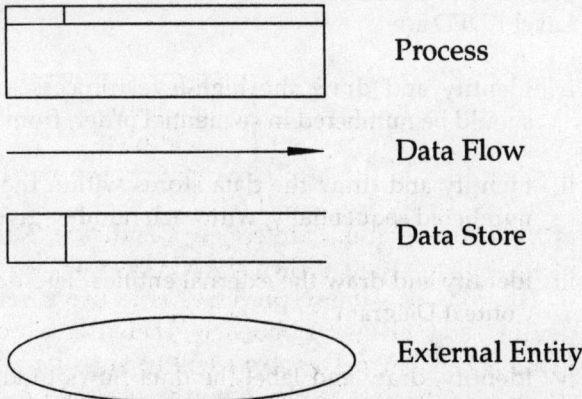

DFDs are constructed using a top-down approach, refining the DFDs into successively more levels of detail. At the top level, a Level 0 DFD, or Context Diagram, is drawn which shows the entire system as a single process with data flows to and from external entities. The steps involved in the creation of a Context Diagram are:

i. Represent the system as a single process box.
ii. Identify and draw the external entities.
iii. Identify, draw and label the data flows between the external entities and the system.

Activity

Draw a Context Diagram for a Student Enrolment System which will contain the processes defined in section 5.2.

The following assumptions have been made for the Student Enrolment System:

i. student applications processing is outside the scope of the system;
ii. students who do not pass the interview will not be notified of rejection.

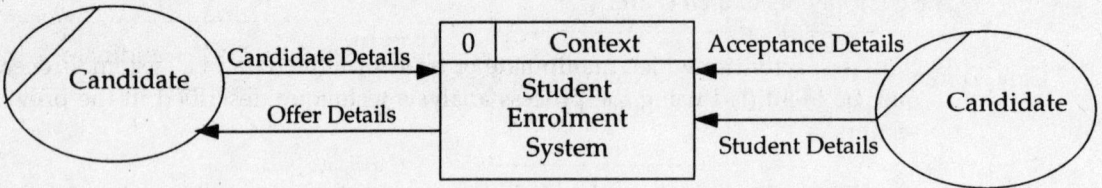

The Context Diagram shows the candidate external entity, the data flows which are sent from it into the system, the data flows which are received by it from the system, and the system itself as one process box. All of the data flows are labelled with the contents of the flow. The line through the external entity identifies that it has been repeated in another part of the diagram. The external entities and data stores of a DFD can be repeated in order to avoid cluttering the diagram and increase the ease of understanding.

Further levels of DFDs will reveal more detail about the system. The process of revealing more detail at each level of DFD is known as *levelling*. The Context Diagram is therefore broken down into a Level 1 DFD which will contain details of the processes and data stores used in the system. The steps involved in the creation of a Level 1 DFD are:

i.   Identify and draw the high-level processes within the system. The processes should be numbered in sequential order, from top to bottom of the diagram.

ii. Identify and draw the data stores within the system. The data stores should be numbered sequentially, with each number given the prefix 'D'.

iii. Identify and draw the external entities. These should correspond with those in the Context Diagram.

iv. Identify, draw and label the data flows to and from the external entities. These should correspond with the data flows identified in the Context Diagram.

v.   Identify, draw and label the data flows between processes and data stores. The arrow head on a data flow indicates the direction of flow. In the case where the data flow is from a process to a data store then data is updated by the process; in the case where the data flow is from a data store to a process, then data is read by the process.

vi. Identify, draw and label any data flows between processes, to indicate that the execution of one process is dependent upon the arrival of data from another process.

Activity

Draw a Level 1 DFD for the Student Enrolment System.

The processes involved in a student enrolment system have already been identified in section 5.2. A Level 1 DFD will only show processes at the same level of decomposition, therefore only the processes Recruit Student, Receive Acceptance and Enrol Student will be shown.

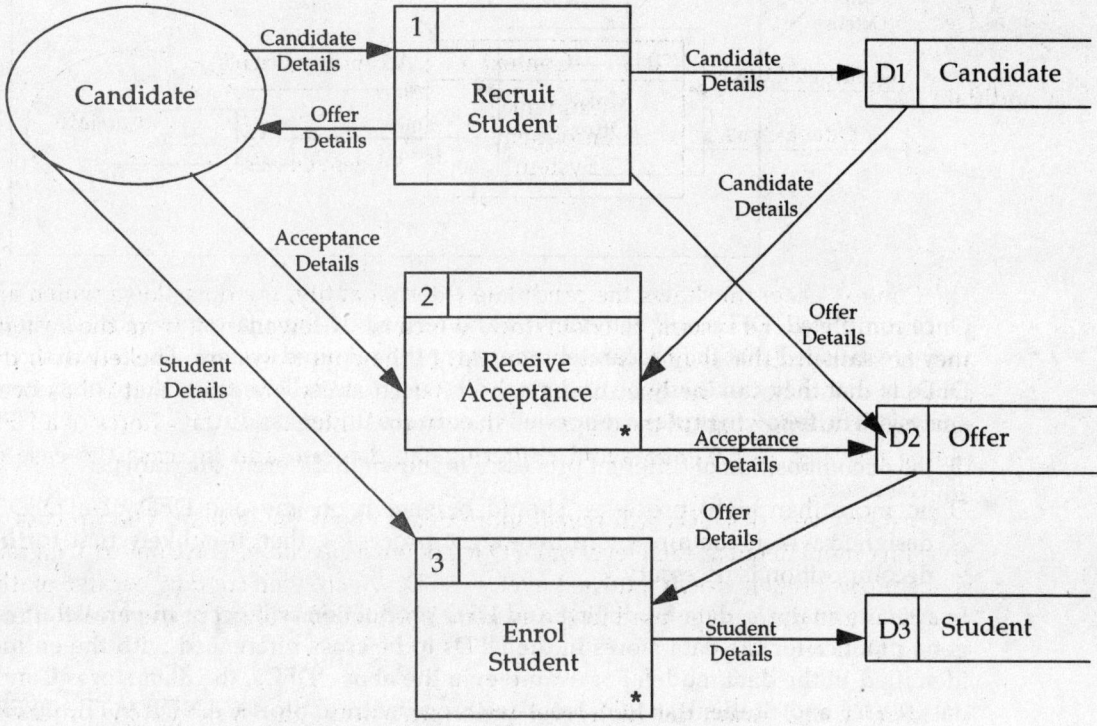

The elementary processes, Receive Acceptance and Enrol Student, are indicated by an asterisk in the bottom right corner of the process box.

Further refinement of the DFD will occur until all of the elementary processes within the system have been specified. Therefore, the process Recruit Student needs to be broken down into a Level 2 DFD. A Level 2 DFD will follow the same steps as a Level 1 DFD. The only difference is in process numbering, where each process is given the number of the process of which it is a further refinement, followed by a decimal point and a number allocated in sequence.

Activity

Draw a Level 2 DFD to further refine the Recruit Student process.

5 Systems Analysis Techniques

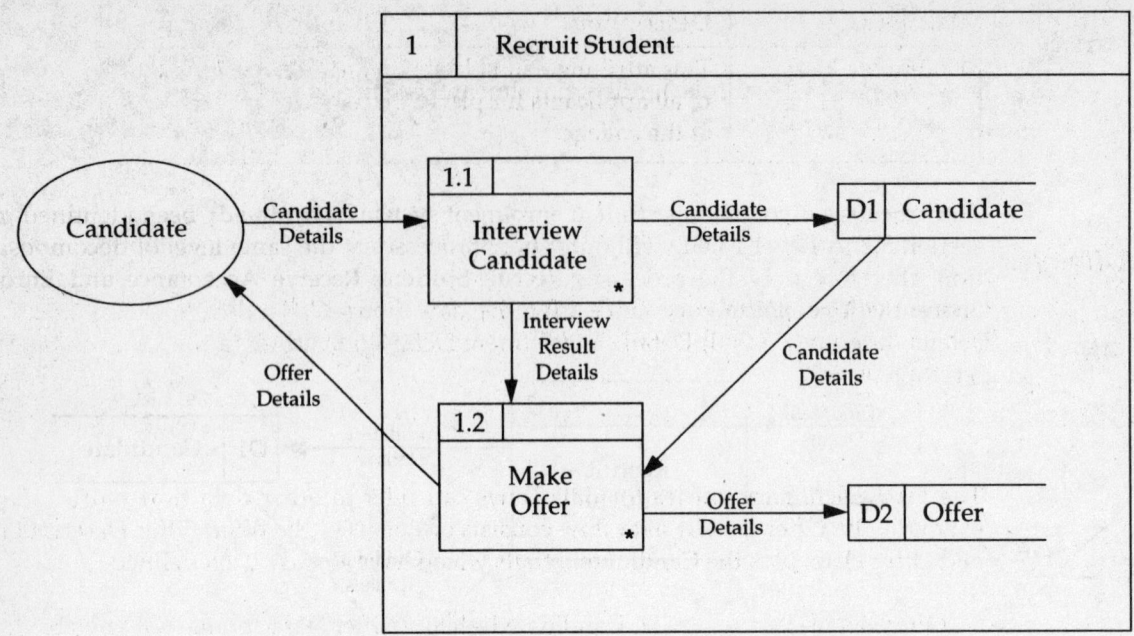

Once completed, DFDs will be reviewed and refined by the analyst and the user until they are satisfied that they accurately represent the required system. The advantage of DFDs is that they can easily be understood by users with little knowledge of systems analysis. The following rules are applied to enhance understanding:

- the decomposition of different processes is shown in different diagrams;
- no more than eight processes should be shown on any one DFD. If a DFD is designed which contains more than eight processes, then it is likely that further decomposition is necessary.

In systems analysis, data modelling and DFD production will occur in parallel. It is a good practice for the data stores in the DFDs to be cross-referenced with the entities identified in the data model. For example, in the above DFDs, the data stores Candidate, Offer and Student should cross-reference with entities CANDIDATE, OFFER and STUDENT which would be identified in the Entity-Relationship Diagram. The DFDs may be reviewed in light of information contained in the Entity-Relationship Diagram, and vice versa.

5.4 Data Dictionary

A Data Dictionary is used to store information about all of the data used in a system. It will contain information about the data flows and data stores in the DFDs, and will also have details of the attributes specified in the data model. With regard to DFDs, the attributes which comprise each data flow will be specified. For example, the data flow Candidate Details, in the DFDs above, might be defined in a Data Dictionary as follows:

  Candidate Details = Candidate Name + Candidate Address +
                Phone Number + Course Name

where Candidate Name, Candidate Address, Phone Number and Course Name would be attributes already defined in the Data Dictionary. The meaning and format of each attribute will also be stored. For example, the following entry describes the attribute Candidate Name:

Attribute	Description	Format
Candidate Name	This attribute will hold the full name of all applicants for places on courses at the college.	CHAR(30)

> *Activity*
>
> Define the Data Dictionary entries for the data flows Offer Details, Acceptance Details, Interview Result Details and Student Details, identified in the DFDs in the pervious section.

The Data Dictionary entries for data flows can refer to other data flow entries. For example, the Offer Details data flow consists of details of the offer, Offer Description and Offer Date, plus the Candidate Details which have already been defined.

    Offer Details   = Candidate Details + Offer Description + Offer Date

The Acceptance Details entry will reference the Offer Details entry, already defined, and Acceptance Date.

    Acceptance Details   = Acceptance Date + Offer Details

The Interview Result Details entry will reference the Candidate Details entry and also contain Interview Date and Interview Result.

    Interview Result Details = Candidate Details + Interview Date + Interview Result

The Student Details entry will reference the Candidate Details entry, and contain the additional information of Date Of Birth and Next Of Kin.

    Student Details   = Candidate Details + Date Of Birth + Next Of Kin

The Data Dictionary ensures the consistency of data between the data model and the DFDs during systems analysis.

5.5 Entity Life Histories

An Entity Life History is a diagrammatic representation of the events in the life of an entity which cause a change to the data stored in the entity. It is drawn as a top-down hierarchical structure, with the entity at the top of the structure, and all of the events which affect it shown at progressive levels. Each Entity Life History represents the life of a single entity from its creation to its deletion. It will show all of the changes which can occur to an entity and relate the changes to the events which cause them. An event is defined as some occurrence which triggers the execution of a process. For example, in the level 1 DFD above, one event is the arrival of the 'Acceptance Details' which triggers the process 'Receive Acceptance'. Each entity identified in the Entity-Relationship Diagram (see Chapter 3), will have its own Entity Life History.

The three main structures used in Entity Life Histories are:

- *Sequence*: represented by a series of boxes which are read from left to right. The first box in an Entity Life History will always show the event which creates the entity, and the last box will always show the event which deletes the entity. The diagram below shows the entity ACCOUNT and the sequence of events in its life.

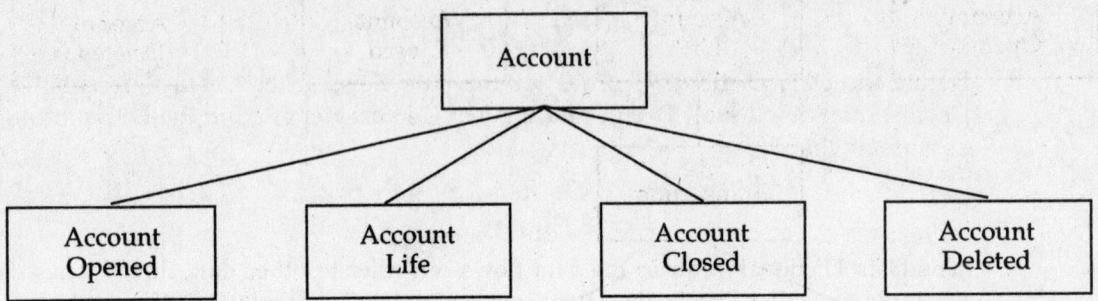

Reading from left to right, an account is opened (creation), it then has an account life, an account may be closed, and finally, a closed account will be deleted at some stage.

- *Iteration*: this occurs when an event may be repeated any number of times. An iteration is represented by an asterisk in the top right corner of the box. For example, the account example can be developed to show that an account life is made up of a number of transactions.

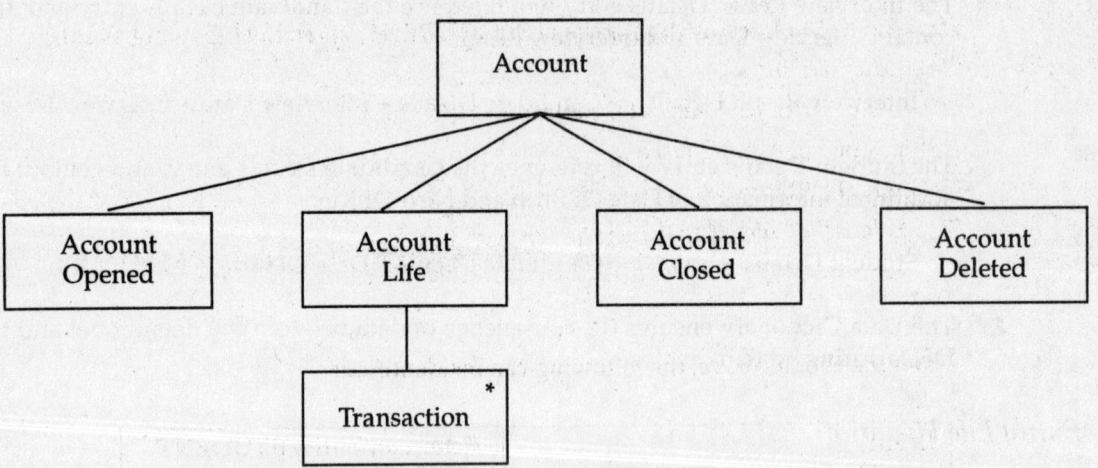

It is possible that an account may be opened and have no transactions made against it, therefore, the event transaction may occur zero or more times. Each occurrence of a transaction will complete before the next one begins.

- *Selection*: this indicates a choice between more than one event. A selection is represented by a circle in the top right corner of the box. For example, if an account transaction may be either a deposit or a withdrawal then the Entity Life History can be expanded to show the selection involved.

5 Systems Analysis Techniques

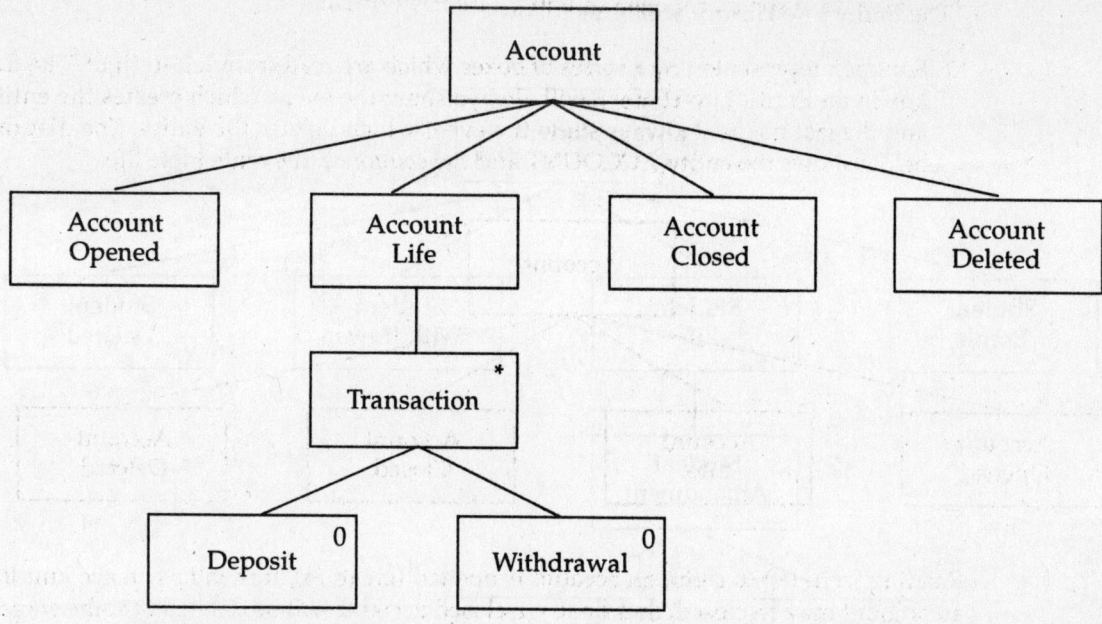

This shows that each transaction which occurs during the life of an account will be either a deposit or a withdrawal.

> *Activity*
>
> Draw an Entity Life History for the entity STUDENT, given the following events:
> - Student Enrols
> - Student Changes Personal Details
> - Student Transfers Course
> - Student Withdraws
> - Student Details Deleted

From the events above, the following can be identified:

Event	Action on Entity STUDENT
Student Enrols	Create STUDENT
Student Changes Personal Details	Modify STUDENT
Student Transfers Course	Modify STUDENT
Student Withdraws	Modify STUDENT
Student Details Deleted	Delete STUDENT

The Entity Life History will be as follows:

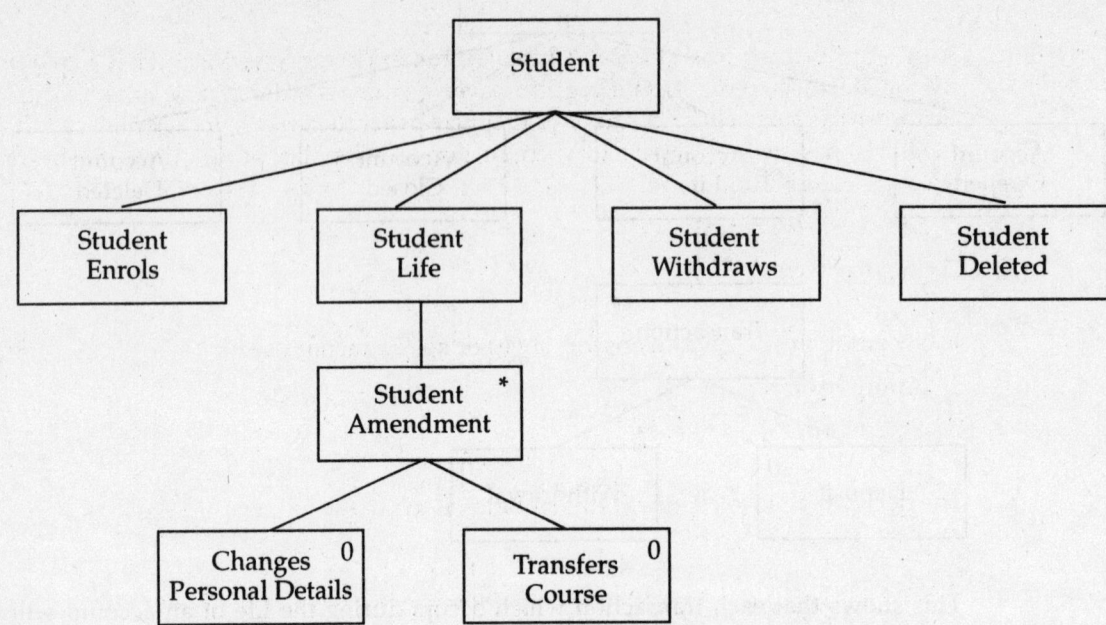

It is important that the analyst ensures the following:

- correlation between the Entity-Relationship Model and the Entity Life Histories by ensuring that each entity has its own Entity Life History.

- correlation between the DFDs and the Entity Life Histories by ensuring that each elementary process in the DFDs which updates a data store is triggered by one or more events in the Entity Life Histories.

5.6 Decision Tables

The systems analyst will have to produce a written description of the processing which occurs in each elementary process identified in the DFDs. The description may just contain a few paragraphs detailing the actions which occur within the process. In some cases, there may be a number of actions which can take place depending on the result of some conditions. If this is the case, then it may be difficult for the analyst to clearly express in text what is taking place, and so an alternative method is used. The common method which is used is to express the conditions and actions as a decision table. Decision tables represent, in a tabular form, any complex series of conditions and actions, which cannot be expressed easily and understandably in a normal written form. They consist of four areas:

- a condition stub contains a list of all possible conditions that can arise during a process;
- an action stub contains a list of all possible actions that can occur within a process;
- a rules area which contains one entry for each possible combination of conditions;
- an action entries area which selects the action to be performed under the specified conditions.

Condition Stub	Rules
Action Stub	Action Entries

For example, consider a process 'Check Customer Credit' which checks if a customer has satisfactory credit, or is a regular payer before an order can be accepted. If the customer has satisfactory credit or is a regular payer then the order is approved. If the customer has neither satisfactory credit nor is a regular payer, then the order is rejected. The conditions are:

- Satisfactory Credit?
- Regular Payer?

Each condition will give an answer of yes or no. The actions are:
- Approve Order
- Reject Order

The decision table to represent this situation is drawn as follows:

	1	2	3	4
Satisfactory Credit?	Y	Y	N	N
Regular Payer?	Y	N	Y	N
Approve Order	X	X	X	
Reject Order				X

This action entries area of the decision table shows that orders are only approved if a customer has satisfactory credit or is a regular payer. If the customer has not satisfactory credit and is not a regular payer then the order is rejected.

Activity

Draw a decision table which represents the scenario that an offer of a place is made to an applicant if they have a good interview and have satisfactory qualifications. The applicant is placed on a waiting list if they have either a good interview or satisfactory qualifications, but not both. The application is rejected if they interview is not good and the qualifications are unsatisfactory.

The conditions check whether the applicant has satisfactory qualifications and a good interview. The actions which can result are either the applicant is made an offer, the applicant is placed on a waiting list, or the applicant is rejected.

The decision table which represents this situation is:

	1	2	3	4
Satisfactory Qualifications?	Y	Y	N	N
Good Interview?	Y	N	Y	N
Make Offer	X			
Waiting List		X	X	
Reject				X

This is known as a limited entry decision table, as it contains only the selectors Y and N in the rules area.

> **Activity**
>
> Draw a decision table which represents the scenario that an offer of a place is made to a student if they have a good interview and if the number of points obtained in their qualifications is greater than 10. The student is placed on a waiting list if they have a good interview and the number of points obtained is between 6 and 10, or if they have a poor interview and the number of points is greater than 10. In all other situations the application is rejected.

The conditions check whether the applicant has sufficient points and a good interview. The actions which can result are either the applicant is made an offer, the applicant is placed on a waiting list, or the applicant is rejected.

The decision table which represents this situation is:

	1	2	3	4	5	6
Qualification Points?	0–5	6–10	11+	0–5	6–10	11+
Good Interview?	Y	Y	Y	N	N	N
Make Offer			X			
Waiting List		X				X
Reject	X			X	X	

This is known as an extended entry decision table as the values in the rules area have values other than Y and N.

The advantages of decision tables are that they can be easily understood by users and analysts, and also it is easy to ensure that all possible conditions are covered.

5.7 Summary

In this chapter we have looked at some of the techniques used in systems analysis. You have seen how function analysis is used to decompose processes to the level of elementary processes. You have examined how DFDs are used to model the required system You have identified the external entities, processes, data stores and data flows in a student enrolment system, and designed the levelled DFDs. You have seen how a Data Dictionary is used to store information about the data to be used in the required system. You have defined the Data Dictionary entries for the data flows identified in the DFDs. You have seen how Decision Tables can be used to express the complex processing which may take place in elementary processes.

Further reading

Clifton, H.D. & Sutcliffe, A.G., *Business Information Systems*, Prentice-Hall

AAT Study Text, *Analysis and Design of Information Systems*, BPP Publishing Ltd

Ashworth, C & Goodland, M, *SSADM A Practical Approach*, McGraw-Hill

Hawryszkiewycz, I.T., *Introduction to Systems Analysis and Design*, Prentice-Hall

Yeates, Don, *Systems Analysis and Design*, Pitman

Exercises

Progress questions

These questions have been designed to help you remember the key points in this chapter. The answers are given at the back of the book.

Complete the following sentences:

1. Process Analysis identifies ....

2. An elementary process is triggered by ....

3. Data Flow Diagrams are used to ....

4. An external entity is ....

5. A Data Dictionary stores ....

6. An Entity Life History is ....

7. Decision Tables are used to ....

8. A process may only be broken down into at least two other processes.

    True ☐ False ☐

9. A Level 1 Data Flow Diagram is known as a Context Diagram.

    True ☐ False ☐

10. The first and last events in an Entity Life History are always creation and deletion.

    True ☐ False ☐

Review questions

>These questions have been designed to help you check your comprehension of the key points in this chapter. You may wish to look further than the text in this chapter to answer them fully. You can check your answers by referring to the appropriate section.

11. Explain the characteristics of elementary processes. (Section 5.2)

12. Explain what is meant by the term levelling. (Section 5.3)

13. Explain how events, needed for the preparation of Entity Life Histories, are identified from DFDs. (Section 5.5)

14. Describe the different control structures which can be used in Entity Life Histories. (Section 5.5)

Multiple choice questions

>The answers to these questions will be given in the Lecturer's Supplement.

15. Which of the following is not a valid process:
    a) Send Invoice
    b) Promote Employee
    c) Update Employee Details
    d) Make Payment

16. Which of the following statements are false:
    a) an elementary process has no subprocesses
    b) an elementary process can be interrupted by another elementary process
    c) an elementary process is normally performed by one person
    d) an elementary process is always triggered by an input from outside the system

17. Which of the following is true:
    a) a Context Diagram shows only external entities and processes
    b) a Context Diagram shows all of the data stores in a system
    c) a Context Diagram shows external entities and the data flows entering and leaving the system
    d) a Context Diagram contains all of the components of DFDs

Practice questions

>A marking guide to these questions will be given in the Lecturer's Supplement.

18. Identify the processes and the external entities in the following:

    'When an order is received from a customer, the stock level is checked to ensure that enough stock is available to fulfil the order. A customer credit check is then carried out on the customer who placed the order. If the stock level and the customer credit level are satisfactory then the order is accepted.'

19. Draw a DFD for the above scenario.

20. Draw the Entity Life History for the following entity/event table:

Event	Action on entity BOOK
Book Purchased	Create BOOK
Book Borrowed	Modify BOOK
Book Reserved	Modify BOOK
Book Returned	Modify BOOK
Book Withdrawn	Delete BOOK

21. Explain why the Entity-Relationship Diagram, the DFDs and the Entity Life Histories must correspond with each other.

22. Draw a Decision Table for the following scenario:

    'A financial institution has to decide upon a course of action whenever a mortgage holder falls into arrears. If the mortgage holder is employed and the arrears are less than £5,000 then the mortgage holder is invited for an interview to discuss the situation. If the arrears are between £5,000 and £10,000 for unemployed mortgage holders, and between £10,000 and £20,000 for employed mortgage holders then three months are allowed to begin paying off the arrears. An unemployed mortgage holder with arrears of over £10,000 is immediately repossessed, an employed mortgage holder with over £20,000 arrears is immediately repossessed.

Questions for advanced students

A marking guide to these questions will be given in the Lecturer's Supplement.

23. The Student Enrolment System, discussed in this chapter, is to have an increased scope. In the area of student enrolment, it will now include also the areas of student applications, taking up of references, and notification of rejection after interview. Apart from student enrolments, the system must now also cover the management of all course details and the management of student attendance on courses. You may use your own experience and investigations to establish the processing requirements for this system. Draw a set of levelled DFDs for this new system which will be called the Course Information System.

24. Describe the Data Dictionary entries for the data flows which you have specified in the DFDs. Draw the Entity Life Histories for any entities which you determine will be necessary.

Assignment

Using the Getwellsoon Hospital scenario and the work you have produced from the previous chapters, do the following:
i. Draw a Context Diagram for the hospital system.
ii. Draw a set of levelled DFDs for the hospital system.
iii. Produce the Data Dictionary entries for each data flow identified in your DFDs.
iv. Draw an Entity Life History for all of the entities which you have identified in the Entity-Relationship Diagram.

6 Detailed Systems Design

6.1 Introduction

This chapter defines the main elements of systems design. On completion of this chapter you should be able to:

- explain the objectives of code design and the characteristics of different coding schemes;
- describe how dialogue design defines the interaction between the user and the system;
- describe the different features which can be applied in screen design;
- describe how Structured English is used in program specifications, and identify the main structures used.

6.2 Code Design

A code is defined as a system of letters and numbers which is used to represent information. A code will always be more concise than the information that it represents. In computer systems, data is often represented as codes rather than as long descriptions, because codes have the following advantages:

- they facilitate computer processing. It is easier for a computer program to recognise and process a code than a text description.
- they save storage space. As a code is shorter than the description it represents, it will occupy less storage space on a computer.

The problem in systems design is to choose a coding scheme which is easily understandable by people, and is precise enough for computer use. For example, in a college or university system, a code of 123 might represent the BSc Computer Studies course, but its meaning cannot easily be deduced from the code. A code of BCS1 would be better, where B refers to BSc, CS refers to Computer Studies and 1 refers to the year of the course.

Activity

What are the requirements of a good coding scheme.

A good coding scheme should meet the following general requirements:

- it must be easy to understand and use;
- it must be capable of expansion to allow for growth of the number of items to be coded;

- it should be brief enough to save storage space on computer and reduce the time taken for system users to input the code;
- it should be designed in a way to minimise the likelihood of errors;
- it must be flexible to allow small changes in classification without necessitating a change to the whole scheme;
- it must provide unique codes for key items such as customer account number;
- it must allow for every item to be coded;

There are a number of different coding schemes available. They include:

- *sequence codes* in which each item is given the next available number in sequence. Sequence codes provide no information about the item which they represent. An example of sequence codes could be:

    1 = sofa

    2 = table

    3 = chair

- *block codes* are used to group items of the same type into groups, with a range of code numbers set aside for each group of items. Code numbers within each group will then be allocated in sequence. The first digit is often used to identify the group classification. For example:

    100 – 199 = sofa
    101 = 2-seater sofa, 102 = 3-seater sofa etc.

    200 – 299 = table
    201 = coffee table, 202 = kitchen table etc.

    300 – 399 = chair
    301 = armchair, 302 = rocking chair etc.

- *significant digit codes* contain digits which are part of the description of the item. For example:

    400 = 486 Personal Computer

    425 = 25 MHz 486 Personal Computer

    433 = 33 MHz 486 Personal Computer

    466 = 66 MHz 486 Personal Computer

- *hierarchical codes* classify items into groups and then break each group into subgroups, and then each subgroup into further subgroups, until the items are coded. A common example of this type of code is the Dewey Decimal Code used by most libraries. For example:

    800 Literature
    　　810 American Literature
    　　　　811 Poetry
    　　　　812 Drama
    　　　　..
    　　　　819 Satire & Humour
    　　820 English Literature
    　etc.

☐ *faceted codes* in which different characteristics of the item are represented by different elements of the code. For example, in a clothes shop items may be represented by the following facets:

    Item Type   Customer Type   Colour   Size   Style

In which the code TRMG3012 would stand for a pair of man's trousers, colour grey, size 30 and style 12 (TR = trousers, M = male, G = grey, 30 = size 30, 12 = style 12). The main advantage of this coding scheme is that it is easily interpreted by the user.

Faceted codes can also be designed to contain only digits, rather than a combination of letters and digits. For example,

☐ *mnemonic codes* in which abbreviations of words are used as the code value. For example:

    LHR = London Heathrow

    LGW = London Gatwick

> *Activity*
>
> Design a coding system which could be used to replace the current sytem of vehicle registrations. The scheme must show the year of registration, the area in which the vehicle was registered and a number which is incremented for each registration during a year.

A possible coding system would consist of three parts:

| the year of registration | the area in which the vehicle was registered | the number of the registration |

Examples of how this system might be applied are:

    1995 L 112   the 112th vehicle registered in London in 1995

    1994 WK 25678   the 25,678th vehicle registered in Warwickshire in 1994

    1995 GN 9   the 9th vehicle registered in Glamorgan in 1995

The code has the benefits of being easy to use and understand. The mnemonic which is chosen to represent the area can be designed to make it as easy to understand as possible.

6.3 Dialogue Design

An on-line system is one in which the user and the system communicate interactively. This interaction is known as a dialogue, and each on-line function of a system will have its own dialogue, designed by systems analysts in co-operation with users. A Dialogue Flow Diagram can be used to show the user-computer dialogue in terms of the exchange of messages. In this context, a message exchange consists of three steps:

i.   The output of information to the user, consisting of screen title, field titles, data values and blank fields for user input.

ii. User action consisting of one or more of, the input of data values, selection of an item from a list, or the pressing of special keys such as function keys or the enter key.

iii. Computer processing of the information entered by the user.

Each message exchange will be given a block in the Dialogue Flow Diagram.

In the previous chapter, an Entity Life History was identified for the STUDENT entity, in which the actions in response to events were identified as creating, updating and deleting student data. In the design stage, the analyst will design the actual on-line function(s) which will allow the system to perform the processing required in response to the occurrence of events. In this case the processing requirements are to allow the user to create students, update students and delete students. Only one on-line function would be required to perform the create, update and delete processing on the STUDENT entity. This function will be called Maintain Student Details, and will have a dialogue designed to allow the user to create a student, update a student's details, delete a student and display a student's details, via a separate screen for each. Most 'Maintain..' functions contain a 'Display Details' component, so it has been added for this case. The Dialogue Flow Diagram is as follows:

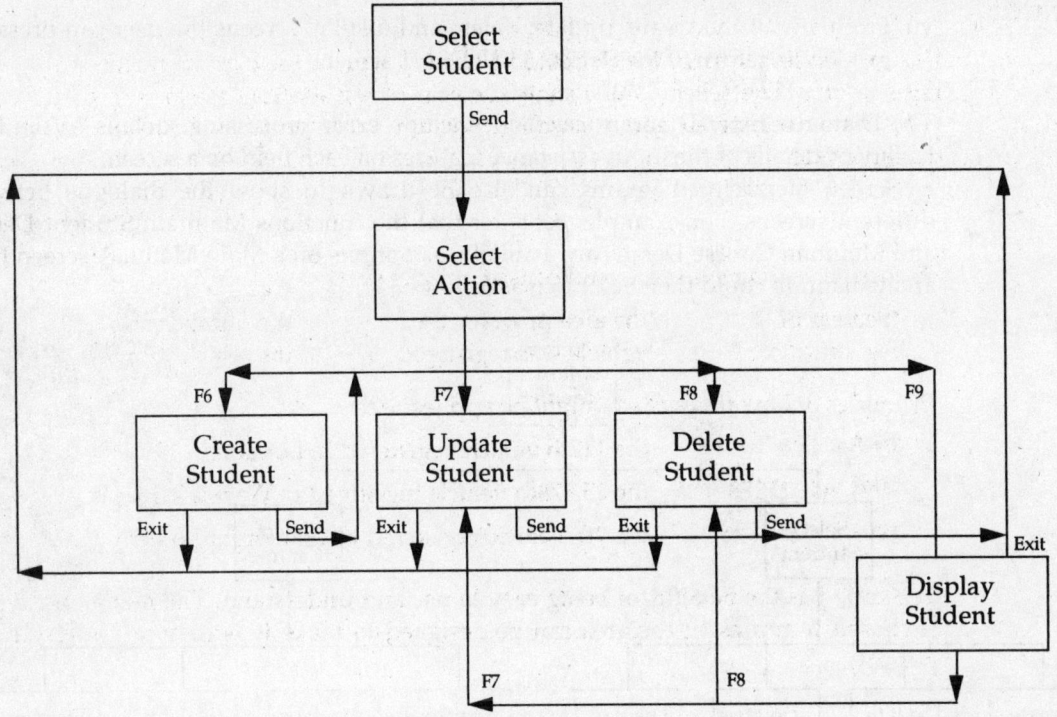

The Dialogue Flow Diagram shows the following sequence of actions once the user has chosen the function Maintain Student Details from a menu:

i. The user is displayed a screen (SELECT STUDENT) which requests the user to input the student number. If the student already exists then the user can input the number. If the student does not exist then the user can press F6 to CREATE STUDENT.

ii. If the user has input a student number, then they can press F7 to UPDATE STUDENT, F8 to DELETE STUDENT or F9 to DISPLAY STUDENT. It should be noted that SELECT STUDENT and SELECT ACTION take place on the same screen.

iii. The computer will process the request and display the appropriate student details on the relevant screen.

iv. From the CREATE STUDENT screen, the user can input the appropriate details and use the enter key to send the information to the database. Upon completion of the send, the create screen will be re-displayed.

v. From the UPDATE STUDENT and DELETE STUDENT screens, the user can input the appropriate details and use the enter key to send the information to the database. Upon completion of the send, the SELECT STUDENT screen will be displayed.

vi. From the DISPLAY STUDENT screen the user can press function key F7 to proceed to the UPDATE STUDENT screen, and F8 to proceed to the DELETE STUDENT screen.

vii. From any of the create, update, delete and display screens the user can press the exit key to return to the SELECT STUDENT screen.

The Dialogue Flow Diagram does not include error processing, details of the help facility or details of the input assistance features on each field on a screen.

Screen hierarchy diagrams can also be drawn to show the dialogue between different screens. For example, consider that the functions Maintain Student Details and Maintain Course Details are available as options on a Main Menu. A screen hierarchy diagram could then be drawn as follows:

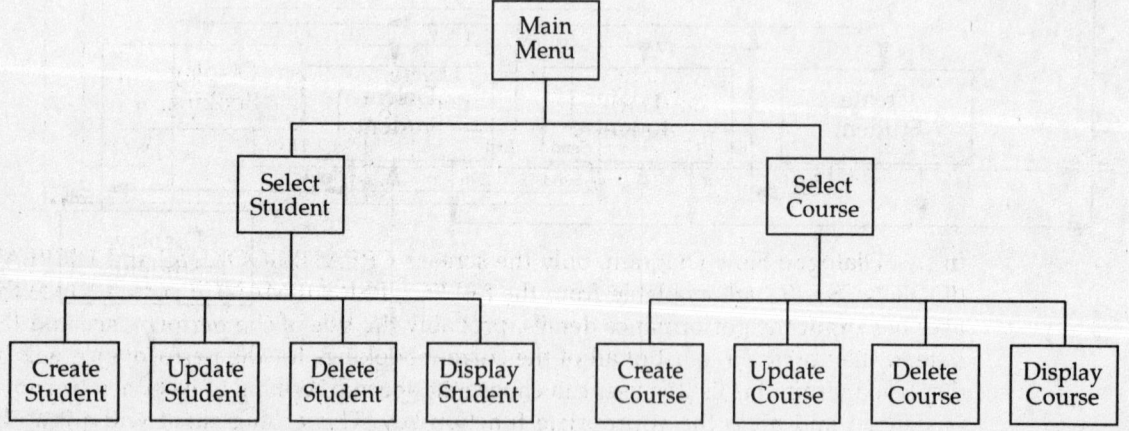

The screen hierarchy diagram could include additional information such as keys which are pressed to move to specific screens, but it is best to avoid cluttering them with too much information. They can then be used to give a simple overview of the system dialogues.

Dialogues can also be designed which allow the user to pass between dialogues rather than simply return back to a menu. For example, before a user creates a student details they may wish to check the course details to see if there are any places available. It would be advantageous if the user could display the course details and then transfer directly to the Maintain Student Details dialogue, rather than having to pass through menus to get from one dialogue to the other. The Display Course screen would therefore need an option to allow the user to do this.

> *Activity*
>
> Design a Dialogue Flow Diagram for a theatre booking system. The dialogue should allow the user to input, amend, delete and display details of bookings for performances.

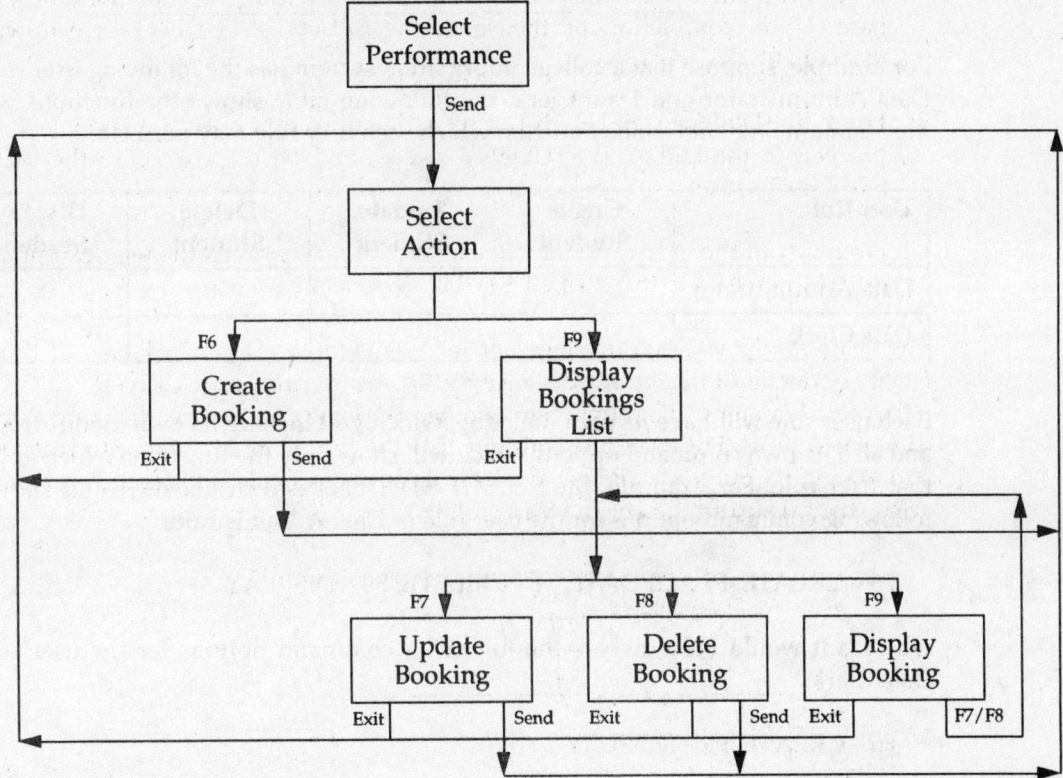

In this Dialogue Flow Diagram, only the screens CREATE BOOKING and DISPLAY BOOKINGS LIST are available from the SELECT PERFORMANCE screen. Once the user has input the performance details, probably the title of the performance and the date, if they press F9, a list of all of the current bookings for the performance will be displayed. From this list the user can choose the specific booking to be either amended or deleted and press the appropriate function key. This arrangement will allow the user to identify bookings without having to key in booking reference numbers, which it is likely the customer may not readily know. The DISPLAY BOOKINGS LIST screen will have to provide sufficient information for the user to uniquely identify a specific booking. From the DISPLAY BOOKINGS LIST screen the user can choose F7 to proceed to the UPDATE BOOKING screen, F8 to proceed to the DELETE BOOKING screen and F9 to proceed to the DISPLAY BOOKING screen. From the DISPLAY BOOKING screen the user can choose F7 to proceed to UPDATE BOOKING and F8 to proceed to DELETE BOOKING.

Each user of a system will not have access to all of the functions within the system, therefore it is necessary to cross-reference the users with the functions which they can perform. SSADM does this by allocating functions to user roles, based on the activities within the organisation which each user role is allowed to perform. A user role may include a number of job titles. For example, the user roles of Data Administrator and Data Clerk could be defined for the following:

User Role	User Job Title
Data Administrator	Senior Administrator Administrator
Data Clerk	Senior Data Input Clerk Data Input Clerk

For example, suppose that a college information system has the following user roles of Data Administrator and Data Clerk, the following table shows the functions within the Maintain Student Details Function which each user role may perform.

User Role	Create Student	Update Student	Delete Student	Display Student
Data Administrator	X	X	X	X
Data Clerk	X			X

Each user role will have its own dialogue, which will include its own menu structure, and also its own command options which will show only the functions which apply to that user role. For example, the SELECT STUDENT screen above would show the following command options for the user role of Data Administrator:

F6 – CREATE, F7 – UPDATE, F8 – DELETE, F9 – DISPLAY

whereas it would only display the following command options for the user role of Data Clerk:

F6 – CREATE, F9 – DISPLAY

6.4 Screen Design

Each screen which is used in an on-line system will be designed by the systems analysts working in close co-operation with the users of the system. All of the screens within a system should have a consistent format, with screen titles, screen prompts etc. appearing in the same location on each screen in the system. The function keys which are assigned to perform certain tasks should also be consistent throughout the system. For example, it is common for the function key F1 to provide the Help facility. Other features such as pull-down menus, colour coding etc. should also be consistent.

Activity

Define a number of general rules which should be followed in the design of screens for a computer system.

The following general rules should be followed:

- only information relevant to the function to be performed should appear on a screen;
- the layout of screens should be consistent throughout a system;
- the use of special keys should be consistent throughout a system;
- screens should not be overcrowded;
- highlighting, colour, flashing, reverse video and sound should be included when appropriate.

The following diagram shows a simple skeleton screen layout, which partitions the screen into specific areas. This skeleton screen would be used as a template for all screens within a particular system, to ensure that things such as screen titles, special key instructions and error messages are always displayed in the same location in each screen.

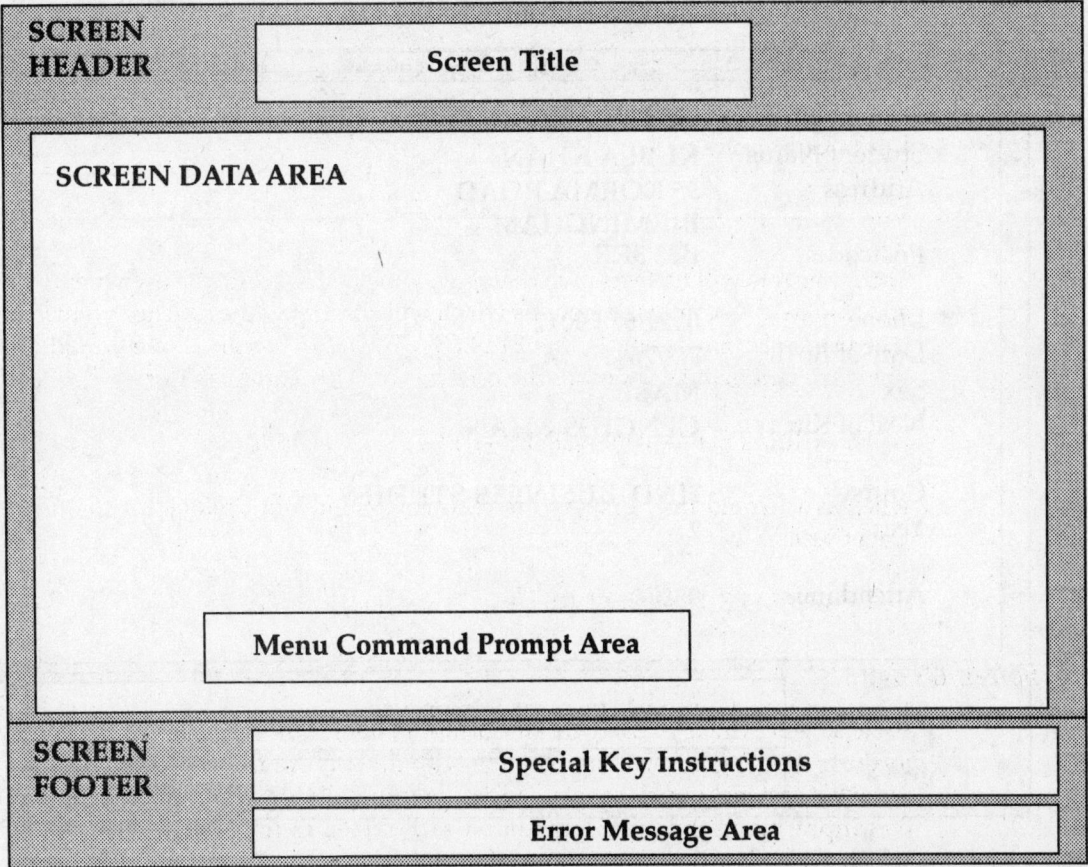

On a screen in which data is to be input by the user, each field on the screen may be allocated one of the following values:

- *Protected and Mandatory*: the field is protected and will always contain data. The user may not enter data or amend the data in any way.

- *Protected and Optional*: the field is protected and may or may not contain data. As it is protected, the user cannot enter data in the field.

- *Unprotected and Mandatory*: the field is unprotected and data must be entered by the user.

- *Unprotected and Optional*: the field is unprotected and the user may or may not enter data into the field.

> **Activity**
>
> Design a screen which allows the user to update details about a student. Identify the fields needed and state which of the above values apply to each field.

```
                    UPDATE STUDENT DETAILS

      Student Number   601574
      Student Name     KUBLA KHAN
      Address          55 KORMA ROAD
                       BIRMINGHAM
      Postcod          B22 3RR

      Phone            0121 678 9012
      Date of Birth    7/3/76
      Sex              MALE
      Next of Kin      GENGHIS KHAN

      Course           HND  BUSINESS STUDIES
      Year             2

      Attendance       95%


      F1-HELP,  Esc-EXIT, Enter-UPDATE
```

All student numbers will be allocated automatically by the system, and once allocated will be protected against change by the user. Once the CREATE STUDENT screen appears, the Student Number field will already contain data, and the user will be unable to change this data in any way. The Student Number field is therefore Protected and Mandatory. The details in the Course and Year fields will probably be obtained from the course table therefore these fields will also be Protected and Mandatory. Any updates to the data in these fields should only be permitted within the Maintain Course Details dialogue.

Each screen which displays student details, may have a field showing the percentage attendance by a student during a course. This figure will be calculated by the system from the information collected from completed registers, and written to the student record. As the value in the field is calculated by the system, it is not desirable for the user to be able to overwrite this value. The Attendance field will be Protected and Optional. Protected because the user cannot overwrite what the system has calculated. Optional because at the start of the year the field will contain a null value as no classes will yet have been run, and therefore no value has yet been calculated.

Each student must have name, address, sex, next of kin and date of birth details specified, therefore these fields would be given the value Unprotected and Mandatory. Whenever a user attempts to create, or update a student, the input will be declared invalid, and an appropriate error message will be displayed if one of these fields does not contain data.

A student may or may not have a phone number and may not know their postcode, therefore the fields Phone Number and Postcode will be given the value Unprotected and Optional. The user may or may not enter data into these fields. The system will not perform any validation checking against the contents of these fields.

Each field on a screen may have special features which assist the user to complete the information required by the field. The following are examples of the special features which may apply to fields:

- *Input Assist* is the mechanism by which the user can identify details about a particular subject without having to input the key field for the subject. For example, if a user wishes to obtain details about a particular student, then they may have an input assist which allows them to input the student name rather than the student number.

- *Cyclic Field* allows the user to cycle through the permitted input values until the required one is found. A simple example would be a field which obtains the marital status of students. Instead of typing one of the values 'single', 'married', 'divorced' or 'widowed', the user could, for example press the space bar until the required value is displayed.

- *Default Values* are contained in fields when they are first displayed, and may be replaced by the user with another value. For example, the default value for the status field may be 'single', and this value would appear in the field each time the screen is displayed.

- *Sort Order* is applied to fields which contain repeating groups. For example, a student may study on more than one course, therefore the courses being studied would appear in course name order.

- *Field Expansion and Playback* are used to allow the user to input a value which is looked up in a table and the table data is displayed on the screen. For example, instead of the user having to type in a full address, field expansion and playback could be applied, in which case the user could enter the post code and the address details for that post code would then be looked up in a table and displayed.

- *Special Validation* can be applied which checks the value in a field against a value previously entered. For example, if the user completes the title of someone as 'Mrs' and then completes the gender field as 'Male', special validation could alert the user to the inconsistency of the data input.

Microcomputer based database packages such as Microsoft Access allow screens to be easily developed using the Forms facility. A form can be set up for the required fields on the database table, and the form can then be used for on-line input. The user can design the form with the help of the FormWizards tool featured in the package.

6.5 Function Design

Function specifications must be written for all of the on-line and batch functions identified. There are no exact rules for identifying functions. The analyst and the user will largely use their own intuition based on experience to decide upon the functions which the system should provide. They must ensure, however, that the following are covered:

- all of the processing performed by elementary processes identified in the DFDs;
- all of the events and actions identified in the Entity Life Histories;
- only the entities and attributes specified in the data model are processed.

Once all of the functions have been identified, it is likely, that the analysts and users will identify the most important functions and develop the specifications for these first. The criteria used to determine the importance of a function are:

- on-line functions which are critical to the running of the organisation;
- on-line functions which are used very frequently;
- major batch functions which are run on a regular basis.

It may be necessary to prioritise functions into a number of different groups and then develop and implement each group in turn.

Each function specification will identify the processing logic for the function concerned. In many cases, the processing logic will be expressed in *Structured English* which has the following characteristics:

- adverbs such as 'however' and therefore' are not used;
- adjectives such as 'tall' and 'old' are not used;
- the control structures used in programming languages to represent sequence, selection and iteration are used.

Structured English is used rather than standard English as it is unambiguous, consistent and concise. For example, the following simple example demonstrates the difference between standard English and Structured English:

English	Structured English
Take a slice of bread and place it on a plate, then take a knife and put butter on the end of the knife and then spread the butter over the bread.	Get slice of bread Place bread on plate Get knife Put butter on knife Spread butter onto bread

The control structures used in Structured English are:

- *Sequence*: a sequence of statements one after the other which are executed in the order in which they occur.

☐ *Selection*: a choice between alternative statements based on the result of a condition. Selection can be represented by IF..THEN..ELSE and CASE constructs:

    IF condition THEN   CASE variable OF
        statement(s)   value : statement(s)
    ELSE   value : statements
        statement(s)   ENDCASE
    ENDIF

For example:

    IF bread is not buttered THEN
        Spread butter onto bread
    ELSE
        Eat
    ENDIF

The same logic can be expressed using the CASE construct:

    CASE bread OF
        buttered : Eat
        not buttered : Spread butter onto bread
    ENDCASE

Activity

Write the Structured English selection statements which check the gender of a student and output an appropriate message in each case.

Using IF..THEN..ELSE:

    IF STUSEX = 'Male' THEN
        OUTPUT 'Student is Male"
    ELSE
        OUTPUT 'Student is Female'
    ENDIF

Using CASE:

    CASE STUSEX OF
        'Male'   : OUTPUT 'Student is Male"
        'Female' : OUTPUT 'Student is Female'
    ENDCASE

☐ Iteration: a sequence of statements is repeated a number of times. Iteration can be represented by the FOR EACH construct:

    FOR EACH entity/variable
        statement(s)
    ENDFOR

For example:

FOR EACH slice of bread
    Place bread on plate
    Get knife
    Put butter on knife
    Spread butter onto bread
ENDFOR

> **Activity**
>
> Write the Structured English iteration statement which outputs the name and address of each student.

FOR EACH STUDENT
    OUTPUT STUNAME, STUADDRESS
ENDFOR

To demonstrate the level of detail required in a Structured English program specification, the following are examples of areas which must be specified in the program specifications:

- all of the processing paths through an on-line function's dialogue must be specified. For example, in the Dialogue Flow Diagram for Maintain Student Details in the previous chapter, each of the options F6, F7, F8 and F9 at the SELECT ACTION stage must be specified.

- all of the actions upon entities, attributes and relationships in the data model must be specified. Examples of actions upon entities are 'Create Entity', 'Read Entity' and 'Delete Entity'.

- all data validation must be specified;

- all conditions which cause error messages to be displayed must be identified;

- all output of messages and screens must be specified.

> **Activity**
>
> Write the Structured English statements to handle the processing of the SELECT STUDENT screen identified in the Dialogue Flow Diagram in the previous chapter. There is no need to be specific about any validation which will be needed.

A basic Structured English specification for this screen would be:

IF INPUT = F6 THEN
    OUTPUT CREATE STUDENT SCREEN
ENDIF
IF INPUT = F7 THEN

```
            READ STUDENT_NUMBER
            PERFORM STUDENT_NUMBER VALIDATION ROUTINE
            READ EACH STUDENT WITH STUNUM = STUDENT_NUMBER
            OUTPUT UPDATE STUDENT SCREEN
         ENDIF
         IF INPUT = F8 THEN
            READ STUDENT_NUMBER
            PERFORM STUDENT_NUMBER VALIDATION ROUTINE
            READ EACH STUDENT WITH STUNUM = STUDENT_NUMBER
            OUTPUT DELETE STUDENT SCREEN
         ENDIF
         IF INPUT = F9 THEN
            READ STUDENT_NUMBER
            PERFORM STUDENT_NUMBER VALIDATION ROUTINE
            READ EACH STUDENT WITH STUNUM = STUDENT_NUMBER
            OUTPUT DISPLAY STUDENT SCREEN
         ENDIF
```

Each student number which is input by the user will have to undergo validation before it is used to find a match in the student table. Each time a student number is input by the user, the same validation will be performed. Therefore, a common routine can be defined to carry out student number validation processing. In the above example, the common routine is the STUDENT_NUMBER VALIDATION ROUTINE.

Computer-Aided System Engineering (CASE) tools usually provide their own Structured English syntax from which computer programs can be automatically generated. In this case the CASE tool will provide an exact syntax for the Structured English which must be strictly adhered to by the systems analysts writing the program specifications.

6.6 Summary

In this chapter we have looked at the main elements in the design of a computer-based information system. You have seen how coding schemes can be designed to reduce the storage space used by a system, and increase the processing performance of the system. You have seen how dialogues are designed to represent the interaction of the user and the system during on-line processing. You have identified the main considerations in the design of screens, and the various features which can be incorporated. Finally, you have examined the use of Structured English in the specification of on-line and batch processing.

Further reading

Yeates, Don, *Systems Analysis and Design*, Pitman

AAT Study Text, *Analysis and Design of Information Systems*, BPP Publishing Ltd

Clifton, H.D. & Sutcliffe, A.G., *Business Information Systems*, Prentice-Hall

Layzell, P, & Loucopoulos, P, *Systems Analysis and Development*, Chartwell-Bratt Ltd

Hill Stephen, *The Human-Computer Interface*, DP Publications, 1995

Thimbleby, H, *User Interface Design*, Addison-Wesley

6 Detailed Systems Design

Exercises

Progress questions

These questions have been designed to help you remember the key points in this chapter. The answers are given at the back of the book.

Complete the following sentences:

1. A coding system saves ....

2. An example of a hierarchical coding scheme is ....

3. A dialogue is...

4. A Dialogue Flow Diagram shows ....

5. Each screen field must have ....

6. The layout of screens should be ....

7. Program specifications must be written for ....

8. A good coding scheme should be flexible and allow for expansion.

   True ☐ False ☐

9. Each user should have access to all of the functions within a system.

   True ☐ False ☐

10. As much information as possible should be displayed on system screens.

    True ☐ False ☐

Review questions

These questions have been designed to help you check your comprehension of the key points in this chapter. You may wish to look further than the text in this chapter to answer them fully. You can check your answers by referring to the appropriate section.

11. Identify the requirements of a good coding scheme. (Section 6.2)

12. Explain how a dialogue can be designed for on-line functions. (Section 6.3)

13. Describe the special features which can be applied to fields on a screen. (Section 6.4)

14. Describe the control structures used in Structured English. (Section 6.5)

Multiple choice questions

The answers to these questions will be given in the Lecturer's Supplement.

15. Which of the following is true:

    a) a faceted code is one in which each item is given a number in sequence

b) a faceted code is one in which each element of the code represents a certain characteristic
c) a faceted code is one in which digits are used that are part of the description of the item
d) a faceted code is one in which items are classified into groups

16. In a screen which allows a user to update customer details:
    a) the customer account number field will be unprotected and optional
    b) the customer account number field will be protected and optional
    c) the customer account number field will be unprotected and mandatory
    d) the customer account number field will be protected and mandatory

17. Field expansion is a feature which:
    a) allows the user to cycle through permitted input values
    b) provides validation checks against previous input
    c) allows the user to input a value which will be used to determine the input for other fields
    d) provides default values in a field when it is first displayed

Practice questions

A marking guide to these questions will be given in the Lecturer's Supplement.

18. Explain what is meant by hierarchical codes.

19. Explain what is meant by a message exchange in an on-line function.

20. Describe the main components of an on-line function which allows a user to Maintain Course Details.

21. Describe the control structures which are used in Structured English.

Questions for advanced students

A marking guide to these questions will be given in the Lecturer's Supplement.

22. Describe an example of a coding scheme which will incorporate some of the features described in Section 7.2.

23. Produce a Dialogue Flow Diagram for an on-line function to Maintain Course Details, which allows the user to pass directly to Maintain Student Details.

24. Identify the fields which will be displayed on a Create Course screen, and, for each one, state whether it is protected, unprotected, mandatory or optional. Also, describe any special features which would be of benefit to completion of the screen.

Assignment

Using the Getwellsoon Hospital scenario and the work you have already produced for the previous chapters, do the following:

i. Identify the on-line functions which the system will need to perform.
ii. Draw a Dialogue Flow Diagram for one of the on-line functions.
iii. Produce a screen design for one of the screens in your Dialogue Flow Diagram. Identify the values which will be applied to each field, and describe any special features which the screen will contain.

Answers to progress questions

Chapter 1

1. Information can be defined as data which has been processed to convey meaning.

2. Information is needed to enable managers to effectively perform the functions of management.

3. The qualities of good information are accuracy, clarity, timeliness, relevance, and frequency.

4. An information system can be defined as a computer-based system which is used to assist in the management and operation of an organisation.

5. A Transaction Processing System is used to process all of the routine transactions generated by the main operations of an organisation.

6. A Management Information System may serve all levels of management to monitor and control the functions over which they are responsible.

7. Each functional area of an organisation will have its own information systems.

8. True.

9. False, it is used at the operational level.

10. False, they are used to solve non-routine and often complex problems.

Chapter 2

1. Hardware is the physical devices that make up a computer system.

2. Software is the computer programs that are executed by the computer.

3. The elements of the CPU are the Control Unit, the Arithmetic-Logic Unit and the Main Store (Memory).

4. The three types of computer are mainframe, minicomputer and microcomputer.

5. OMR is used in multiple choice exams and in the National Lottery.

6. The classes of printer are character printer, line printer and page printer.

7. The main backing storage media are magnetic disk, floppy disk, magnetic tape and optical disk.

8. False.

9. False, it is an example of systems software.

10. False, MICR is used for cheque processing.

Chapter 3

1. The main types of file in a traditional file system are master files and transaction files.

2. A database is an organised collection of data that can be accessed by many users and used for many purposes.

3. A Database Management System controls data storage, data retrieval, access to the data and data security.

4. The Database Administrator is responsible for the design of the logical database and the building of the physical database.

5. A logical data model is a design of the database; an Entity-Relationship Diagram is an example of a logical data model.

6. External views are used to restrict access to only those areas of the database which are actually required.

7. An entity is something of interest to the organisation about which data needs to be stored.

8. False.

9. False.

10. False, the E-R Diagram should be refined to remove all many-to-many relationships, and those one-to-one relationships in which the participating entities share most of the same attributes.

Chapter 4

1. A methodology is a collection of stages, procedures and techniques which assist the development of computer-based information systems.

2. Systems development methodologies adopt a structured and formal approach to systems development.

3. The feasibility study determines whether or not a project is viable and should proceed.

4. The principal objective of systems analysis is to produce a detailed specification of the requirements for the new information system.

5. Systems analysis concentrates on what processing needs to be carried out by the new system, and what data is needed for the system to perform that processing.

6. Systems design concentrates on how the system will perform the processing that is required.

7. The main stages in programming are design, code and test.

Answers to Progress Questions

8. False, interviews are the most common.

9. True.

10. False, it is the most risky.

Chapter 5

1. Process Analysis identifies the processing that needs to be done by the new system.

2. An elementary process is triggered by the arrival of an input, the completion of another elementary process, or a specific time being reached.

3. Data Flow Diagrams are used to model systems by showing the data flows, the processes and the data stores within the systems.

4. An external entity is the source of data entering the system, or the recipient of data which has left the system.

5. A Data Dictionary stores information about all of the data which is used in a system.

6. An Entity Life History is a diagrammatic representation of the events in the life of an entity from its creation until its deletion.

7. Decision Tables are used to represent complex logic, involving a number of conditions and actions, in a tabular form.

8. True.

9. False, a Level 0 DFD is known as a Context Diagram.

10. True.

Chapter 6

1. A coding system saves storage space and processing time.

2. An example of a hierarchical coding scheme is the Dewey Decimal Code used in libraries.

3. A dialogue is the communication between the user and the information system, expressed as a series of screens and commands.

4. A Dialogue Flow Diagram shows the user-computer dialogue in terms of an exchange of messages.

5. Each screen field must have a value allocated; the possible values are: protected and mandatory, protected and optional, unprotected and mandatory, unprotected and optional.

6. The layout of screens should be consistent throughout a system.

109

Answers to Progress Questions

7. Program specifications must be written for all of the on-line and batch functions identified during systems design.

8. True.

9. False, a user should only have access to those functions which are required to perform their job role.

10. False, screens should not be overcrowded with information.

Index

Access Methods 2.6
Arithmetic-Logic Unit (ALU) 2.2
Attribute 3.5, 4.5, 5.4

Bar Coding 2.3
Batch Processing 1.4
Block Code 6.2
Byte 2.6
Byte 2.6

CASE Tool 4.3, 6.5
Central Processing Unit (CPU) 2.2
Changeover 4.8
Check Digit 2.4
Code Design 6.2
Communications Devices 2.2, 2.7
Composite Key 3.5, 3.6, 3.7
Computer Misuse Act 4.8
Context Diagram 5.3
Control Unit 2.2

Data 1.2
Data Capture 2.3
Data Dictionary 5.4
Data Flow 5.3, 5.4
Data Flow Diagram 5.3, 5.5
Data Independence 3.4
Data Modelling 5.2
Data Processing Manager 4.2
Data Protection Act 4.8
Data Redundancy 3.2, 3.4
Data Store 5.3
Data Validation 2.4
Database 3.2, 3.3
  advantages of 3.4
  physical database 3.7
Database Administrator (DBA) 3.4, 4.2
Database Management System (DBMS) 3.3
Decision Support System (DSS) 1.3, 1.7

Decision Table 5.6
  extended entry 5.6
  limited entry 5.6
Dialogue Design 4.6, 6.3
Dialogue Flow Diagram 6.3
Direct Access 2.6
Distributed System 2.7

Elementary Process 5.2
End-User Computing 1.4
Entity 3.5
Entity Life History 5.5
Entity-Relationship Diagram 3.5, 5.5
Exception Reporting 1.4
Executive Information System (EIS) 1.3, 1.8
External Entity 5.3
External View 3.3

Faceted Code 6.2
Feasibility Study 4.4
File Conversion 4.8
File System 3.2
Foreign Key 3.5, 3.7
Form Design 4.6
Function Design 6.5

Hardware 2.2
Hash Total 2.4
Hierarchical Code 6.2

Implementation 4.8
Indexed-Sequential Organisation 2.6
Information 1.2
  qualities of 1.2
  internal 1.2
  external 1.2
Information Engineering 4.3
Information System 1.3
Input Devices 2.2, 2.3
Internet 2.7
Iteration 5.4, 6.5

Key Field 3.2, 3.5

Local Area Network (LAN) 2.7
Logical Model 3.3

Magnetic Disk 2.6
Magnetic Ink Character Recognition (MICR) 2.3
Magnetic Tape 2.6
Main Store 2.2
Mainframe 2.2
Management 1.3
Management Information System (MIS) 1.3, 1.5
Master File 3.2
Matrix Code 2.3
Microcomputer 2.2
Minicomputer 2.2
Mnemonic Code 6.2
Modem 2.7
Multiplexor 2.7
Multiprocessing 2.2
Multiprogramming 2.2

Normalisation 3.6

Office Automation System (OAS) 1.3, 1.6
On-line Processing 1.4
Operating System 2.2
Operational Management 1.3
Optical Character Recognition (OCR) 2.3
Optical Disk 2.6
Optical Mark Reading (OMR) 2.3
Output Devices 2.2, 2.5

Parallel Running 4.8
Pilot Operation 4.8
Printer 2.5
Process 4.5, 5.2, 5.3
Process Analysis 5.2
Programmer 4.2
Programming 4.7

Index

Project Steering Group 4.2, 4.3
Protocol 2.7
Prototyping 4.9
RAM 2.2
Relationship 3.5

Screen Design 4.6, 6.4
Screen Hierarchy Diagram 6.3
Selection 5.4, 6.5
Sequence 5.4, 6.5
Sequence Code 6.2
Sequential Access 2.6
Significant Digit Code 6.2

Software 2.2
  applications software 2.2
  systems software 2.2
SSADM 4.3, 6.3
Storage 2.2, 2.6
Strategic Management 1.3
Structured English 6.5
Structured Query Language (SQL) 3.7
Systems Analysis 4.5
Systems Analyst 4.2
Systems Design 4.6
Systems Development Life Cycle 4.3

Systems Development Methodology 4.3

Tactical Management 1.3
Terminal 2.5
Terms of Reference 4.4
Time-sharing 2.2
Transaction File 3.2
Transaction Processing System (TPS) 1.3, 1.4
Turnaround Document 2.3

Virtual Storage 2.2
Visual Display Unit 2.5

Essential Elements

covering the core of modular courses

Further titles in this series...

Essential Elements of
Management Accounting *Jill & Roger Hussey*

Contents: The role of management accounting; Cost classification and control; Total costing; Marginal costing; Capital investment and appraisal; Budgetary control; Standard costing; Appendices.

ISBN 1 85805 103 7

Essential Elements of
Financial Accounting *Jill & Roger Hussey*

Contents: The accounting framework; Users and uses of financial information; The cash flow forecast; The profit and loss account for a sole trader; The balance sheet for a sole trader; The financial statements of a limited company; Interpretation of financial statements.

ISBN 1 85805 091 X

Essential Elements of
Business Economics *Mark Sutcliffe*

Contents: The UK economy – an overview; Resource allocation; Business costs; The structure of business and its conduct; Small firms and multinationals; Wages and the labour market; Investment, R & D and training; National economic change and business activity; Money, banking and inflation; Economic policy and the business environment; The international dimension; Europe and business.

ISBN 1 85805 095 2

Essential Elements of
Human Resource Management *Sally Howe*

Contents: An introduction to human resource management; The organisational context; Human resource planning and administration; Employee resourcing; Equalising employment opportunities; Employee development; Reward management; Employee relations.

ISBN 1 85805 145 2

All titles in this series are approximately 128 pages long, and measure 275 x 215mm.

Essential Elements
covering the core of modular courses

Further titles in this series...

Essential Elements of
Business Statistics *Les Oakshott*

Contents: Survey Methods, Presentation of data, Summarising data, Probability and decision making, The Normal Distribution, Analysis and interpretation of sample data, Testing a hypothesis, Correlation and regression.

ISBN 1 85805 104 5

Essential Elements of
Quantitative Methods *Les Oakshott*

Contents: Index numbers, Investment appraisal, Time series analysis, Linear programming, Critical path analysis, Stock control methods, Simulation.

ISBN 1 85805 098 7

Essential Elements of
Marketing *Roderick Smith*

Contents: What is marketing?, The product, Promotion, Selling as part of marketing, Pricing policy, Place and distribution, Marketing research, Marketing management.

ISBN 1 85805 102 9

All titles in this series are approximately 128 pages long, and measure 275 x 215mm.

Tackling Coursework
Projects, Assignments, Reports and Presentations

David Parker

This book provides the student with practical guidance on how to approach the coursework requirement of a typical business studies course, i.e. projects, assignments, reports and presentations. The text makes clear the different approaches needed for the different types of coursework, with examples of each in an Appendix, and there is advice on how to conduct research, collect information and present results, in either written or verbal form. It is expected to be used on the following courses: any business studies course at undergraduate (e.g. BABS) or postgraduate (e.g. MBA) level. It would also be useful as a preparatory text for a research degree.

Contents:

Introduction, Dissertations and projects, Essays and papers, Management reports, Seminars and presentations, Research methods. **Appendices:** *Further reading, Example of a dissertation proposal, Example of citations, Dissertation contents, Example of an essay.*

1st edition • 96 pp • 215 x 135 mm • 1994 • ISBN 1 85805 101 0